"Leroy Spinks has written a heartfelt and convincing argument that salvation in the New Testament is not founded on a legal theory, but on a family relationship. He effectively argues that the primary metaphor used by Jesus and the early church is God as a loving Father, and that atonement is reconciliation within a family, not a legal transaction. He describes how Christianity suffered a 'great amnesia' about the loving Father, and how medieval concepts of honor and satisfaction came to shape Christian thinking. In a book that remains very readable, Spinks marshals biblical and historical knowledge to sustain his argument."

Stephen Finlan
, The First Church
Bridgewater, Mass.

"Leroy Spinks writes as a pastor-theologian. As a pastor, he describes what Christian laypersons today believe about the meaning of Jesus' death and the prominence of penal substitution in their understanding. As a theologian, he interprets the many diverse biblical teachings about Jesus' sacrifice and surveys what other theologians have written about it across twenty centuries. He offers a brilliant, powerful thesis of his own: God our loving Father has pursued us, his prodigal children, all the way to the cross in order to bring us back into his family where he works to transform our lives and through us to transform the world. I recommend this wonderful book enthusiastically. I hope it will give all of its readers an enriched appreciation for the good news that 'Christ died for our sins according to the Scriptures.'"

Fisher Humphreys
Professor of Divinity Emeritus
Samford University

"In this carefully documented and well-written book, Leroy Spinks argues persuasively for the rejection of the notion that Jesus had to be punished on the cross for the sins of humanity. Appealing to Old Testament metaphors of God as liberator and redeemer of Israel, Spinks argues that the contribution of Jesus and his followers was the understanding of God as the personal liberator and redeemer of individuals as well. He presents the reader with a God who forgives our sin and rebellion, not because of the cross, but despite it, and draws us into a safe and loving family. I recommend this volume for serious adult Bible study groups."

Sharyn Dowd
Retired New Testament scholar and pastor
Decatur, Ga.

"I, like Leroy Spinks, grew up in a Christian home with a loving father and mother. As a child I learned 'for God so loved the world that he gave his only begotten Son, that whosoever believeth in him shall not perish, but have everlasting life.' I believed that as a child and still do. I must admit that I have really never delved into explanations of the atonement in any detailed way. My life has been filled with medical/surgical training and then later a busy practice of thoracic and cardiac surgery. But throughout the years, I have never lost sight of the wonderful realization that God loved me enough to send his Son—for me, and for everyone else! In this book I found the thorough descriptions of various theories of the atonement to be extremely interesting. Especially enlightening are the historical explanations of the differing concepts. The sidebar charts are well done and helpful in recapitulating the information presented in short form, making it easy to rethink what I had just read in orderly fashion. It gives me great comfort and peace of mind to realize fully that the Father—my Abba—sent his Son to reconcile all of us unto himself."

Joel Avery
Retired cardio-thoracic surgeon
Chattanooga, Tenn.

"Finding traditional explanations of the atonement, particularly the penal substitutionary theory, both unhelpful and unfaithful to the teaching of Jesus, Leroy Spinks sets out to develop an understanding of the atonement based on Jesus' life and teachings. Focusing on such things as Jesus' relationship with God as represented by his use of *Abba* and the Hebraic near-kin redeemer model, he offers fresh insights into the meaning of the cross. All who desire a deeper understanding of the atonement will find this book of interest."

Hulitt Gloer
Professor Emeritus of Preaching and Christian Scripture
George W. Truett Theological Seminary, Baylor University

"Leroy Spinks has provided a spirited argument against the current, prevailing atonement theory that portrays Jesus' crucifixion as an act of propitiation of God the Father. Spinks maintains that the development of this theory can be traced from its roots in the 'Great Confusion' of the second and third centuries and through medieval feudalism, Anselm's satisfaction theory, and Calvin's thought concerning penal substitutionary atonement. In contrast, Spinks argues that Christians should understand the atonement as Jesus proclaimed and lived it, as the means of reconciliation to a loving, heavenly Father in alignment with the Father's deliverance of Israel from slavery in Egypt and exile in Babylon. Written for lay folk, this book covers a great deal of ground and presents a welcome, critical voice among today's theological ideas."

Jim McConnell
Associate Professor of New Testament Interpretation
Gardner-Webb University School of Divinity

Abba, Father
VIEWING ATONEMENT THROUGH THE JESUS LENS

Leroy Spinks

© 2020
Published in the United States by Nurturing Faith, Macon, GA.
Nurturing Faith is a book imprint of Good Faith Media (goodfaithmedia.org).
Library of Congress Cataloging-in-Publication Data is available.

ISBN: 978-1-63528-124-8

All rights reserved. Printed in the United States of America.

All Scripture citations are from the New Revised Standard Version (NRSV)
unless otherwise indicated.

Cover photo: Wesley Tingey/Unsplash

Contents

Acknowledgments vii

Introduction 1
The Church's Struggle with the Atonement

Chapter 1 9
A Clue Hidden in Plain Sight

Chapter 2 17
Let My People Go

Chapter 3 23
Depending on Kinfolk

Chapter 4 29
Redeemed from Exile

Chapter 5 37
The Gospel According to Jesus

Chapter 6 51
The First-century Church

Chapter 7 69
Migration Away from Jesus' Good News

Chapter 8 75
Anselm's Satisfaction Theory

Chapter 9 83
Calvin's Penal Substitution Theory

Chapter 10 91
Penal Substitution Today

Chapter 11 101
Tying Up Loose Ends

Conclusion 107
When Cultures Collide

Appendices 115
Redemption Vocabulary in the Old Testament 115
Redemption Vocabulary in the New Testament......119
Glossary..126
Bibliography 127

Acknowledgments

Abba, Father, for me, is a group project. So many people have graciously read the manuscript as it developed and given their critiques and suggestions—most of which have been incorporated into the final result—that I can never repay their assistance.

- I thank first of all my wife, Annette Spinks, for her reading and correcting the manuscript with the eye of an experienced English teacher and my ever-present editor and encourager.
- My cousin and dear friend Tony Baker, a published poet and songwriter and recorded performing artist, critiqued the manuscript with the eye of the well-read layman and the soul of a poet.
- My good friend Tom Prevost, pastor and missionary, made several insightful observations as a serious student of the Bible and a deep theological thinker.
- Joel Avery, a retired cardiovascular surgeon, read the manuscript and critiqued it from the viewpoint of an intelligent layman who takes his faith seriously and studies the Bible in depth.
- Finally, I wish to thank Baptist scholars and theologians Fisher Humphreys, Dalen Jackson, Sharyn Dowd, and Hulitt Gloer and United Church of Christ theologian and scholar Stephen Finlan, whose incisive critiques have enabled me to sharpen the final work considerably.

All these friends have contributed much to this work, and to them I am forever indebted. Of course, I have to take responsibility for the flaws in the final product, for none of them would endorse every opinion I have expressed here.

***

I wish to dedicate this work to the First Baptist Church of Chattanooga, the Waters Sunday School class, and our pastor Dr. Thomas Quisenberry, all of whom provided much emotional and spiritual support and inspiration during the writing of this manuscript.

Introduction

The Church's Struggle with the Atonement

A Haunting Sermon Illustration

Our revival preacher was in full evangelistic pleading voice as I sat on the right end of the second pew from the front beside my cousin and aunt. He had mastered the use of his voice to touch the emotions of his audience, and he certainly could stir our feelings. His flaming oratory mesmerized this twelve-year-old kid.

"Let me tell you a story from the American frontier," he intoned. "Little Johnny was caught stealing a pencil from another student. Mr. Thompson, the teacher, told Johnny to take off his shirt for the beating he had so rightfully earned. When Johnny took off his shirt, the class gasped at his skinny back, his ribs and backbone showing through his pale skin. What would Mr. Thompson do?

"At that moment Billy stood up," the evangelist continued. "Tall. Rugged. Well built. 'I'll take his beating, Mr. Thompson.'

"So, Billy took off his shirt, laid down across little Johnny, and took the ten licks from Mr. Thompson's cane across his bare back." The preacher paused, looking at each of us as his story sank in. "And that is what Jesus did for each and every one of you." The evangelist's voice practically wept with emotion.

I am sure many an eye in the congregation filled with tears as the preacher completed his story. We could all identify with Johnny's relief at not having to take the beating. We could all admire Billy's courage in taking Johnny's beating for him. This child, however, felt overwhelming revulsion. I identified with Johnny. I admired Billy. But the teacher horrified me. If Johnny represented us, and Billy represented Christ, then the teacher represented God!

"What kind of teacher would do any of that?" I thought in horror. "And I'm supposed to believe God is like that? No sirree, Bob! The God I know and love is not like that. My God is not cruel—not even in the name of justice."

From that moment on, I rejected the way our preachers frequently presented the gospel—not the gospel itself, but the way they sometimes told the story. Of course, most of the time they preached simply the love, mercy, and grace of God given us in Jesus Christ. On the other hand, when they devoted a sermon to explaining how Christ's death provides forgiveness of sin, they always reverted to the second version as represented in the above story with its horrible image of Christ taking our punishment from God to make it possible for God to forgive us. That version is possibly how you have frequently heard the gospel preached, too.

A Positive, Encouraging Gospel

We never hear in my present church the kind of preaching described above. In our church, we only hear the positive, encouraging gospel of the love of God extending to everyone, offering God's grace to all who will receive it. Many believers have always been a part of churches preaching the positive gospel our pastor and church proclaim. These Christians do not identify with my childhood experience. Still, the terrible vision of someone having to die to pay God back for our sin has had a negative effect even on the thinking of this latter group without their necessarily realizing it. Even in our more positive version of the gospel, there remains something of a hole in our theology.

What do we do with the Easter season? That period in the church year focuses on the death of Jesus Christ by crucifixion. But what is the significance of that death? Each time we observe Communion (the Lord's Supper), we "proclaim the Lord's death until he comes" (1 Cor. 11:26). Why does the church regularly, repeatedly celebrate the *death* of Jesus? Many Christians wear an ornamental cross around their necks to signify their faith in the cross of Christ. Roman Catholic Christians regularly make the sign of the cross as a symbol of their faith. The Greek letter *chi* (which looks much like our English letter "X") has long been a symbol for Jesus Christ. It comes from the twin facts that the first letter of "Christ" in Greek is *chi* and the Greek cross was shaped like that letter.

An ancient symbol of Christianity is the *chi-rho*—the Greek letters *chi* and *rho*—superimposed over one another. This symbol represents both the first two letters of Christ in Greek and the shape of the Greek cross. This symbol, which goes back at least to the time of Constantine, regularly appears in church banners. Many churches have a Roman cross affixed to the wall somewhere in their worship sanctuary.

Why is the Christian faith so full of representations of the cross on which Jesus died? What other religion or national group celebrates as the center of its culture the *death* of its founder—particularly the tortured *execution* of its founder as a criminal? Christianity does not just commemorate Jesus' grisly death; we celebrate it and glory in it. That singular characteristic of the church is at least curious, is it not? Our theology should offer some explanation of that unique trait of our faith.

The theology inculcated into us as children contained an explanation for the death of Christ celebrated in Communion and Easter. Jesus literally took our place, we were told. He paid our sin debt. He died for our sin to make it possible for God to forgive us and make us his children. Having given up that theology, what do we put in its place? How do we now explain the salvation Jesus Christ proclaimed and brought to humankind, now symbolized by the cross?

Introduction

Questions

Having rejected the version of the gospel that so repulsed me as a child, I settled into a simple faith that God loves us and saves us through Jesus Christ. Precisely how he does that and what part Jesus' death plays in that salvation, though, has long sat uneasily in my mind. Even having rejected the theology of the cross of my rearing, the gospel of the terrible wrath of God demanding a death to pay for Adam's sin—for which we are guilty—continued to stalk the recesses of my mind.

As the atheist Richard Dawkins asks in *The God Delusion*, "If God wanted to forgive our sins, why not just forgive them, without having himself tortured and executed in payment?"[1] Like Dawkins, although a disciple of Jesus Christ, I found myself asking the same question. Reportedly, in his early life Dawkins was educated in Anglican schools. Surely, he did not hear in the Church of England that fundamentalist theology of my childhood. So, what was the source of Dawkins' haunting question? Possibly it came from the lack of a clear answer to the question, "Why did Jesus die to bring us God's forgiveness and salvation?"

I have always known that my experience of God came through Jesus who died on the cross. Still, I could not adequately explain how Christ's death provided atonement with God. Early in adulthood, having come to understand the nature of the Bible as presented in my previous book *The Jesus Lens*, the fundamentalist theology of my childhood and youth fell behind.[2] Still, that original question loomed: "How did Jesus provide atonement for the human race?" Merely abandoning one theology without putting something better in its place did not entirely satisfy. Through the years I have preached many of the basic ideas in this book, but I was still plagued with the feeling that I did not have a biblical basis for my theology of the cross.

Two Intriguing Conversations

While some people may think the theology that repulsed me as a child is totally a thing of the past, these ideas continue to crop up even now.

A young veterinarian attended the Sunday morning worship service of our church and then invited me out for breakfast. Thinking he was about to join or wished to discuss my sermon, I was thrilled. Soon after sitting down with him in the restaurant, he startled me with the accusation of not teaching my people properly. "Your Sunday School teachers don't even know the meaning of the word 'propitiation,'" he charged. It turns out he had challenged the teacher of the class he attended to define the word "propitiation" in 1 John 2:2 (King James Version). Of course, the teacher could not. That proved I was failing my people.

I responded, "Well, I don't know why he should know that word. It isn't a very important word in the New Testament."

He protested indignantly that it is the most important word in the New Testament and all of theology, to which I replied that it and similar words and concepts rarely occur in the New Testament, and two of the rare occurrences of the Greek word in the New Testament actually mean "mercy seat." The other two times are in the little book of 1 John; and even there, the Greek word does not mean "propitiation." It is hardly a major New Testament idea. This young professional insisted that someone has to pay God back for the debt we have incurred by our sin. Someone has to "propitiate" God—appease him, placate him—assuage his anger at our sin against him and his law.

Several years later I was serving in another church on the other end of the state. A young medical doctor invited me out for breakfast after attending our Sunday morning worship service. Exactly the same conversation took place, almost word for word. Interestingly, both these young professionals had moved to these locations from the same major church in a university town of our state. I suspect they had been trained there to do exactly what they had both done—confront pastors not preaching that archaic theology and show them the error of their ways.

An Advertising Door Hanger

Recently someone from a local church left a professionally designed and produced advertising piece hanging on our front door knob, inviting us to their worship services. The photograph on the card showed a smiling, attractive pastor with his wife and children. The quality of the flyer shows this pastor and his church care enough to do things first class. That someone took the time to place invitations on the doors of strangers shows they care about the spiritual welfare of their community. Most striking, however, was their statement of faith. Titled "You Can Have A Personal Relationship with God through Jesus Christ," their statement had five bulleted points.

- Realize God loves you.
- Realize everyone is a sinner.
- Realize sin has a price that must be paid.
- Realize Jesus Christ died and rose again to pay for your sin.
- Pray and ask Jesus Christ to be your Savior.

Now, who could quarrel with the title of that advertising piece? Everyone yearns for a personal relationship with God, or the Eternal, or Ultimate Truth—however an individual may express it. The first point on the door-hanger thrills. The love of God absolutely holds center place in the gospel according to Jesus. Who could disagree with the second point? A person does not have to be a biblical scholar or a theologian to recognize that our entire world is messed up. We see human sin and evil everywhere—in international affairs; in national, state, and local government; even in churches and families. What is more, if we examine our own actions, motives, and desires, we recognize that the line of ignorance and evil of our world runs straight through every heart—even our own.

Then, there's that third point. Does this pastor realize he ultimately received it from a priest born, reared, educated, and conditioned in medieval feudal Europe and England nine hundred years ago? Does he have any comprehension that Archbishop Anselm designed this statement of the Christian faith to communicate with a people almost a millennium ago barely out of pagan superstition? And what about that fourth point? There's nothing about God seeking lost children and nothing about Jesus, the embodiment of God, calling us back into God's family. That point focuses only on paying God back the suffering and pain we deserve because we dissed God's honor, or justice, or righteousness, or holiness (whichever this pastor focuses on). Here we are face to face with *propitiation* again.

This young pastor is no doubt a wonderful husband, father, pastor, and friend. Certainly, beyond any shadow of doubt, he loves Jesus and the Bible as the word of God. Without having met him, he appears a likeable pastor and friend. His theology, however, does present a problem for many people. He did not draw it from the Bible. More importantly, he did not learn it from Jesus Christ. The brochure his church distributes is a current example of the force of pagan law and tradition having crept into the church and Christian theology nine centuries years ago.

It's Hard to Escape This Theology

Max Lucado, pastor of the Oak Hills Church in San Antonio, Texas, has thrilled readers for years with his uplifting books on the gospel of Jesus Christ.[3] Lucado presents Christ in a positive, refreshing way. He has for the most part abandoned the old theology; but even he cannot totally escape the 900-year impact of the old tradition. Even Lucado retains something of Anselm's and Calvin's satisfaction theories, in spite of himself, in writing of God's having been "appeesed" by the death of Christ, for example.[4]

Not everyone who accepts Calvin's penal substitutionary view of the atonement proclaims it in quite the plain, unvarnished manner presented here. Still, when we hear talk of "paying our sin debt" or "satisfying God's justice," we can know the speaker holds that old theology. When we hear preachers intoning on "the wrath of God," we can frequently suspect that old theology of the atonement lurks in the background. When theologians or ministers speak of the atonement producing some effect in God, or enabling God's forgiveness, they show they have been influenced by this way of thinking. It appears that most ministers, laymen, and especially hymnists no longer truly believe this old way of proclaiming the cross, but few of us can escape its influence entirely. An editor of a religious journal recently commented that the issue of the atonement continues to haunt many non-fundamentalist ministers as well as laymen.

A Beloved Old Hymn

This old theology chases us into every by-way and alley no matter how hard we try to escape it. The evidence jumped out recently from that beloved old hymn "What Wondrous Love is This." This work of gorgeous music and captivating poetry shocked me as we sang the first two stanzas.

> What wonderous love is this, O my soul, O my soul!
> What wonderous love is this, O my soul!
> What wondrous love is this that caused the Lord of bliss
> To bear the dreadful curse for my soul, for my soul,
> To bear the dreadful curse for my soul.
>
> When I was sinking down, sinking down, sinking down,
> When I was sinking down, sinking down,
> When I was sinking down beneath God's righteous frown . . .

"Bear the curse? Sinking down beneath God's righteous frown?" No matter how you try to explain away that theology, it is still Anselm and Calvin coming at us with a terrifying medieval picture of God and the atonement. And it showed up in a hymnal in which almost none of the hymns know such a horrible conception of God. We find it difficult to escape this idea that has plagued the church for almost a millennium.

A Fresh Look at Atonement

In *Abba, Father: Viewing Atonement through the Jesus Lens*, I set out to rethink atonement in a departure from what is possibly the most popular theory among conservative Christians. This book reexamines atonement by giving careful attention to the words of Jesus. It abandons entirely the concept of "the atonement" held as the most popular view among conservative evangelicals today.

Most of the classic theories of the atonement proposed what the authors intended to be literal, often legal, explanations of what Jesus did for us on the cross.

Introduction

One of the older popular theories dating back to the third and fourth centuries proposed the literal, legal explanation that Jesus paid a ransom to the devil for our souls. Several centuries later Anselm proposed the literal, legal theory that Jesus made satisfaction (paid God compensation or reparations) for our offense to God's honor. Several centuries after that, the Reformer John Calvin proposed that Jesus paid our sin debt for our offense to God's justice. (Chapters 7, 8, and 9 will trace the history of these theories.) Mention of the classical theories of the atonement refers to these three theories (plus another discussed briefly in chapter 7). These theories proposed the idea that the cross of Christ provided "the atonement"—an event that made it possible for God to forgive us and make us his children.

The New Testament shows that Jesus did not preach any "theory of the atonement." In fact, Jesus never used any word that could be translated "atonement," nor did he preach any concept that could be so construed. Jesus proclaimed the metaphor of the loving Father. Jesus taught how we are to reconcile (although he never used that word, either) with the Father, not how the Father reconciles himself to us. In addition, the message of all the New Testament authors following Jesus continued this theme while also offering many other metaphors illustrating how Jesus brings us back to God. The view presented here does not claim to be Jesus' theory of the atonement, for the New Testament evidence does not indicate that he had one. Instead, the following chapters will develop what Jesus proclaimed as his Good News of the kingdom of God. Once we understand the gospel Jesus preached, we do not need any theory of the atonement. Jesus' message as communicated through his favorite metaphor stands sufficient on its own.

The obsession of much of the church with the concept of the atonement represents a departure from Jesus' own message. This analysis of Jesus' teaching, therefore, will speak only of "atonement" in the sense of our "reconciliation" to God, not of "*the* atonement"—an event that made it possible for holy God to accept us into his family. This work will develop these ideas in the hope that by the end of the book the reader will grasp a new conception of the message Jesus proclaimed.

This book is not intended to be a study of the doctrine of the atonement. The following chapters will not explore all the different theories of the atonement, assessing their strengths and weaknesses. It is not even designed as a study of New Testament teaching on the atonement. You will not find in these pages a study of Paul's or Peter's doctrine of the atonement. To go even further, this book is not even a study of Jesus' doctrine of the atonement, for he never approached that subject. Jesus never uttered the word "atonement" or any other word that can be translated that way. "The atonement" is *our* obsession that first arose during the second century and afterward and came to hold center place in church theology from about 1100 CE onward.

This book addresses one single issue: What did Jesus teach relevant to our obsession with the atonement? Until we can ascertain what Jesus said relevant to atonement, we are not ready to discuss the wider issue of New Testament teaching on that subject or to build a church doctrine of atonement.

The approach adopted here will present some readers with problems of translation into today's idiom. We must first understand Jesus' teaching, however, before attempting to translate it into a mode of expression that resonates today. Chapter 11, "Tying Up Loose Ends," will deal with the problems Jesus' message presents some people today and translate it into a manner of speaking that communicates with our contemporaries.

Notes

[1] Richard Dawkins, *The God Delusion* (Boston: Houghton Mifflin, 2006), 253.
[2] Leroy Spinks, *The Jesus Lens* (Macon, GA: Nurturing Faith, 2018).
[3] For example, Max Lucado, *No Wonder They Call Him the Savior* (Nashville: Thomas Nelson, 2004).
[4] Ibid., 27.

Chapter 1

A Clue Hidden in Plain Sight

Jesus preached the Good News of our loving Abba.

Searching for a Place to Start

For years I attempted unsuccessfully to understand exactly how Jesus and his crucified death save us. In time, I settled into the solution many ministers and laymen apparently have chosen: God has saved us through Jesus Christ, even if we cannot explain it. Simple faith had to cover my ignorance. For several decades I preached out of the wonderful insights and ideas presented by Fisher Humphreys in his book *The Death of Christ*.[1] Still, I yearned for a more specific understanding of the atonement, something firmly based in the explicit teaching of the New Testament.

Then one day a new thought dawned: How did Jesus see the salvation he proclaimed and effected? That question led to another problem. An examination of Jesus' teaching revealed he never seemed to actually give any systematic teaching on the atonement. He never even uttered the word "atonement" or any other word that could be so translated, according to the New Testament record. The very idea of "the atonement" seemed to be foreign to Jesus' thinking and preaching. That word names our obsession inherited from two thousand years of church history. Then what did Jesus imply by what he did teach? That question led to the view presented in the remainder of this work.

Jesus' Words in His Native Tongue

You have heard it said that the Old Testament was written in Hebrew and the New Testament in Greek. Although Jesus apparently knew both tongues, he probably did not speak either language most of the time. He spoke Aramaic as his native tongue. He probably did read Hebrew, for Luke records that he read the Scriptures in the synagogue at Nazareth. He no doubt did speak Greek when dealing with foreigners in the marketplace. At home and among his friends and followers, however, he would have spoken Aramaic. After all, that was the contemporary local language.

It may surprise you to learn that we only have four word-for-word quotations of Jesus in the entire New Testament. Every other quotation of Jesus in the Gospels is a Greek translation of what Jesus actually said in Aramaic. Mark alone of the gospel writers quoted Jesus in his native tongue—and even then, in only four brief snippets. (These snippets hold tremendous significance, however, as we will see in Chapter 5.) When Matthew, Luke, and John told those same stories, they always translated Jesus' Aramaic words into Greek for the benefit of their readers. Here are those four verbatim Aramaic quotations—all in the Gospel of Mark:

1. On one occasion a synagogue leader asked Jesus to come to his home and heal his critically ill twelve-year old daughter. On the way to his house, a messenger came to tell the father his daughter had died. Undeterred, Jesus went on to Jairus' house. Ignoring the scoffing of the mourners already there, he entered the girl's room. Then he said to her, "Little girl, get up." Well, that is Mark's translation of what he said. Jesus actually said in Aramaic, "*Talitha koum!*" (Mark 5:41).

2. On another occasion he healed a man who could neither hear nor speak plainly. Jesus put his fingers in the man's ears and touched the man's tongue with his own spittle and said to him, "Be opened," as Mark translates him. The actual command in Aramaic was, "*Ephphatha!*" (Mark 7:34).

3. As Jesus hung on the cross, he cried out, "*Eloi, Eloi, lema sabachthani?*" (Mark 15:34). His cry meant, "My God, my God, why have you forsaken me?" The Greek-speaking bystanders, not understanding Aramaic, thought he called out for Elijah to save him, when actually he called out an agonizing question to God.

4. The only other time Mark records Jesus as speaking Aramaic occurred the night before his crucifixion, the evening prior to the quotation cited in the previous paragraph. He and his disciples left the place where they had observed the Passover seder and retreated to their camp in Gethsemane. There Jesus led his band of followers into an all-night prayer session. Eventually, Jesus moved away from his disciples to pray in privacy. Kneeling in prayer, he cried out to his heavenly Father, "*Abba!*" (Mark 14:36). Mark reported Jesus' cry like this: "*Abba*, the Father." The evangelist did not mean that Jesus prayed "*Abba* the Father." Mark meant that he prayed, "*Abba*"; and *Abba* means "the Father."

These are the only four word-for-word Aramaic quotations from Jesus to come down to us. The last cited of these presents a clue to Jesus' own teaching relative to atonement. To unpack that clue, however, requires some meticulous thinking about that piece of evidence.

Paul and the Jesus Tradition

About two decades after Jesus' crucifixion and resurrection, the Apostle Paul wrote a letter to the church of Galatia. In that epistle he wrote, "Because you are sons, God sent the Spirit of his Son into our hearts, the Spirit who calls out, '*Abba*, Father'"

(Gal. 4:6). Those last two words in Paul's Greek read literally, "*Abba*, the Father"—as Mark quoted Jesus in Gethsemane—even down to the unusual details of the Greek spelling.² Five or ten years later, Paul wrote to the church at Rome: "For you did not receive a spirit that makes you a slave again to fear, but you received the Spirit of sonship. And by him we cry, '*Abba*, Father'" (Rom. 8:15). As in his letter to the Galatian churches earlier, Paul's Greek read, "*Abba*, the Father"—exactly the way Mark quoted Jesus, even to the Greek spelling.

When Matthew and Luke quoted Jesus' prayer in Gethsemane, on the other hand, they neither quoted his Aramaic *Abba*, nor did they quote him as praying to "the Father." Instead, Matthew quoted Jesus as praying, "my Father," in Greek (Matt. 26:39, 42). Luke, on the other hand, quoted Jesus as praying simply, "Father" (Luke 22:42). On top of these differences, both Matthew and Luke changed Mark's spelling of "Father," thereby correcting his grammar.

The Meaning of Paul's Statement

Mark reported that Jesus prayed "*Abba*, Father" in the Garden of Gethsemane. Paul did not actually write of Jesus' praying "*Abba*, Father." He wrote of *the church of his day, two to three decades after Jesus*, praying "*Abba*, Father." Paul's comment indicates that the way Jesus spoke of God had become the language of the first-century church at prayer and worship.³ The ancient church in Paul's day decades after Jesus still echoed him in Aramaic. Clearly, they saw something critically important in the way Jesus spoke of God. What was that significance? Why did the way Jesus referred to God resonate so with the early church?

The Significance of These Quotations

Matthew and Luke dropped Mark's *Abba* and quoted Jesus as praying in Greek "Father" (Luke) or "my Father" (Matthew).⁴ Mark and Paul, however, repeated faithfully exactly what came to them in the oral tradition, even though the traditional quotation and translation did not reflect precisely correct Greek grammatical usage. Paul and Mark both recognized a deep significance in the oral tradition of Jesus' Aramaic address to God and quoted it verbatim. Their independent citations of the oral tradition suggest that Jesus' calling God *Abba* constituted a highly meaningful part of his teaching that survived for decades in the memory and public worship of the early church.

Mark's quotation of Jesus and Paul's citation of the early church could be a clue to understanding Jesus' gospel and teaching relative to atonement. Jesus regularly referred to God and prayed in his native Aramaic in a way not ordinarily practiced by his contemporaries. His word *Abba* did not represent the equivalent of our word "Daddy," as is frequently asserted. That word *Abba*, however, spoken without a modifier such as "in heaven" did ring too familiar for the religious leaders of his people. The intimacy of Jesus' teaching about the Father does not rest in the bare definition of the word *Abba* but in the way Jesus and the first-century church used it.[5]

What *Abba* Signified

Prior to Jesus, only rarely did anyone in the Hebrew Scriptures or other Jewish writings refer to God as "Father" or "my Father."[6] Occasionally someone did call God "our Father," meaning the Father of the people of Israel. Yet, when Jesus referred to God as his own personal Father, whether in Aramaic or Greek, his manner of addressing God or speaking about God sounded far too intimate for his Jewish contemporaries. Similarly, when he said God was their Father, that terminology also sounded far too familiar and irreverent to them. They recognized God as Israel's Father but not their own personal Father as individuals. With this way of referring to God, Jesus had gone too far for many of his countrymen, especially for the Sadducees (the Temple authorities) and the Pharisees (the lay teachers of the Scriptures).

The word *Abba* represented the language of a child or an adult speaking to his or her father. Used alone, that word carried something of the connotation of "my father." Possibly that is why Matthew regularly added personal pronouns to "Father" in quoting Jesus—to indicate that Jesus' usage represented a more personal reference to God than usual. When we observe how Jesus used this term in his Gethsemane prayer, we notice that he was in great anguish of soul as he cried out to his Father. Paul actually used the word "cry out" in both passages where he quoted it of church usage. Crying out in emotional and spiritual agony in itself implies some level of intimacy between the supplicant and God.

Furthermore, Jesus cried out to his *Abba* from a life devoted to his Father, out of long experience with God. His cry was not that of childish immaturity and ignorance but of deep experience of the love and faithfulness of his gracious Father gained from years of personal relationship. Similarly, in both of his uses of this word, Paul said we cry out to God as "adopted" children of God, indwelt by God's Spirit who enables us to cry out in this way.

In Romans, Paul went on to say that Jesus has become the "firstborn among many brothers and sisters" (Rom. 8:29, author's translation). We, too, are now individually the children of God and together the family of God. To call God *Abba* testifies to our experience of having been adopted into God's family. We therefore know ourselves to be brothers and sisters of Jesus himself and of one another.

Jesus and His *Abba*

The Gospel According to Luke preserves what is probably the favorite of all Jesus' parables.[7] In this story, the younger son takes his inheritance long before the father's death and wastes it in wild living. Then a famine hits the land where he has ended up. The young man finds himself not only broke but so degraded he is slopping hogs for a Gentile farmer. How much lower could a young Jew sink? In desperation, he decides to go back home where possibly he can get a job as a hired hand on his father's farm.

The father, however, has been eagerly watching for the return of his lost boy, sees him coming a long way off, and rushes out the greet him. The young man does not get to deliver the speech he has carefully constructed to win his dad's heart, for his father grabs him in a bear hug and announces he is throwing a party—a barbeque. The father does not care about restoration of the material wealth he has lost. He does not care about compensation for his son's disrespect of his honor. He just wants his precious boy back.

Many preachers and theologians insist we cannot draw theological conclusions from this story. Why not? That claim says this story tells us nothing about God. Then why did Jesus waste his time and that of his hearers telling it? Why did Luke place it at the center of his gospel? Why do we waste time preaching it? Luke's placement of this story at the center of his narrative suggests it contains an encapsulation of Jesus' concept of his message about his Father.

This story along with Jesus' preaching in general implies that atonement is all about reconciliation, fellowship, communion between parent and child—and nothing else. Atonement means restoration of fellowship—not compensation for lost honor, or wounded justice, or insulted righteousness, or offended holiness. (We will examine these ideas and their origins in chapters 8 and 9.) The father's heart is love above all else—above justice, or righteousness, or holiness. God's justice is loving justice. God's righteousness is loving righteousness. God's holiness is loving holiness. Love is primary. Love is the dominant attribute of God. That truth constitutes Jesus' Good News—the heart of the Father is love.

Do I make too much of this story? After all, since it only appears in Luke's gospel, could it possibly be as important as I have made it? True, this one story appears only in Luke. The emphasis on the love of the Father, however, appears throughout Jesus' teaching in all four gospels and in all the New Testament following the gospels. In all the New Testament gospels Jesus' teaching can be summed up in his message of the loving Father.

Take the Sermon on the Mount (Matthew 5–7) as an example. You have probably heard your pastor preach that in the Sermon on the Mount Jesus proclaimed the kingdom of heaven. Yet, Jesus referred to his Father more than twice as many times in the Sermon on the Mount as he referred to the kingdom.[8] It seems we have missed the major point of the Sermon. In that message, Jesus did not announce primarily the kingdom but the Father. Or maybe we should say Jesus proclaimed the Father's kingdom—with the major emphasis on the Father. Possibly we could even go so far as to say the Good News of the kingdom of God is the Good News of the family of God. God's kingdom is his family.

One Sabbath, Jesus encountered a lame man and healed him. The religious authorities reacted with rage. After all, did not their law forbid working on the Sabbath—even healing? Jesus responded to their outrage, "My Father is still working, and I also am working" (John 5:17). Then the evangelist reported, "For this reason the Jews were seeking all the more to kill him, because he was not only breaking the sabbath, but was also calling God his own Father, thereby making himself equal to God" (v. 18).

Although John's gospel is the only one to record this story, all four evangelists agree that the Sanhedrin condemned Jesus to death because he regularly called God his Father, with the implication that he was the Son of God.[9] Matthew and Luke both recorded Jesus' startling statement, "All things have been handed over to me by my Father; and no one knows the Son except the Father, and no one knows the Father except the Son."[10] This quotation from Matthew and Luke echoes the way the Gospel of John records Jesus as speaking constantly. Jesus' supreme offense (among many) to the Jewish authorities, according to all four gospels, resided in the highly personal way he repeatedly referred to God as "my Father," *Abba*.[11]

Now, however, we face a critically important question.

Why Didn't Jesus Say *Abba* More Often?

If the fact that Jesus called God his *Abba* held such significance, why didn't he say it more often than that one time in Gethsemane? He did, many scholars conclude.

The evangelists who reported Jesus' teaching always translated his Aramaic words into Greek, except for the four times Mark alone reported his words in Aramaic. Read through the gospels and notice how often Jesus spoke of the Father, my Father, your Father, our Father, or their Father. The fact that Jesus spoke Aramaic, combined with the citations of Mark and Paul, suggests that every time we read of Jesus' referring to God as Father, he used the Aramaic word *Abba*. The evangelists, however, translated his Aramaic into Greek, because many or most of their readers did not understand Aramaic. For this reason, our English translations always represent Jesus as saying Father except for the single time Mark quotes him as praying *Abba*.

As a matter of historical fact, Jesus probably usually, maybe always, spoke of God as *Abba*.[12] This constant usage by our Lord as suggested by Mark's narrative of Gethsemane provides a clue to Mark's understanding of Jesus' gospel. This clue has been lying there all along—hidden in plain sight. Jesus' teaching about his Father sounds so familiar to our ears that we have failed to recognize that single word as the heart of the gospel Jesus preached. Still, the significance of Jesus' gospel does not reside solely in the Aramaic word *Abba*. Had he simply referred to God as "my Father" in Greek, even that way of expressing himself would have rung far too familiar and therefore offensive to his Sadducee and Pharisee hearers.

The Heart of Jesus' Gospel

The heart of this book can be stated in a single sentence: Jesus lived and preached the Good News that our loving Abba calls us back to himself, asking only that we receive his forgiveness and fellowship. There is much more, of course, in Jesus' preaching concerning the life he called us to live in fellowship with the Father. Most of Jesus' teaching concerned the character of the life to which God calls us. The Good News of the Father, however, held center place in Jesus' gospel. Jesus preached the Good News of reconciliation with our loving Father, not placation of an angry deity.

A Question

Focusing on Jesus' constant reference to God as his Father, your Father, our Father—as *Abba*—raised another question: How could Jesus' calling God *Abba* possibly have moved first-century Jews so powerfully? For those of us who have had strong, loving fathers, that image resonates powerfully. Is it possible, though, that in Jesus' first-century culture that image held an even deeper significance than our twenty-first-century picture of a father? What deeply held cultural concepts among the Hebrew people could have given Jesus' favorite word for God resonance in communicating his gospel?

The multiple profound answers to this question will occupy the next three chapters and will provide the cultural context and connotation of the gospel according to Jesus. Please understand, however, that the material in the next few chapters does not represent Jesus' message but merely the cultural background of his message that gave it emotional power for his original hearers. His metaphor of atonement was God as *Abba*; the next three chapters present the cultural context of that metaphor that gave it such emotional power.

Notes

[1] Fisher Humphreys, *The Death of Christ* (Nashville: Broadman, 1978).

[2] ο Πατηρ (*ho pater*; pronounced HO PAH-TAYR), nominative case (as in Mark and Paul) in Greek is spelled the way a Greek speaker pronounced and spelled the subject of a sentence.

[3] Gerhard Kittel even suggests that Mark's and Paul's formulation may reflect early liturgical usage in the church, possibly even the way the church began the Lord's Prayer in public worship (*Theological Dictionary of the New Testament*, Grand Rapids: Eerdmans, 1964), 1:6. See also Gottlob Schrenk, πατηρ, *Theological Dictionary of the New Testament*, Gerhard Friedrich, ed., Geoffrey W. Bromiley, trans. and ed. (Grand Rapids: Eerdmans, 1967) 5:984-990; James D.G. Dunn, *Word Biblical Commentary: Romans 1–8*, (Dallas: Word, 1988), 461; and Richard N. Longenecker, *Word Biblical Commentary: Galatians* (Dallas: Word, 1990), 175.

[4] Πατερ (*Pater*, pronounced PAH-TER), vocative case (as in Matthew and Luke) is spelled the way a Greek speaker pronounced and spelled the word when addressing his or her father directly. In the vocative case, however, the speaker did not include the definite article "the" as Mark and Paul did in translating *Abba* into the Greek nominative case.

[5] Sigve Tonstad presents this case persuasively in his article "The Revisionary Potential of 'Abba! Father!' in the Letters of Paul," Andrews University Seminary Studies, vol. 45, 1, 5-18 (Berrien Springs, MI: Andrews University Press, 2007). Compare also these two quotations from eminent scholars: "Jesus' use of [Abba] was not unique, nor did it necessarily imply a unique sense of divine sonship, but it was distinctive, perhaps even somewhat unconventional" (Craig Evans, *Word Biblical Commentary: Mark 8:27–16:20*, vol. 34B [Nashville: Thomas Nelson, 2001], 412). On the other hand, John Nolland expressed the following opinion: "Despite dissenting voices, Jeremias' judgment stands that Jesus' own reference to God as 'my Father' or 'Abba' . . . is without parallel in ancient Palestinian Judaism" (*Word Biblical Commentary: Luke 9:21–18:34*, vol. 35B [Dallas: Word, 1993], 613).

[6] Ps. 89:26, 103:13; Mal. 2:10; and Tobit 13:4 in the Apocrypha are almost exceptions to this rule, but not quite the same as Jesus' assertions. A few other exceptions have been cited in Jewish works in Greek and also in the Dead Sea Scrolls, but these examples are rare and truly exceptional.

[7] Luke 15:11-31.

[8] Jesus mentioned the kingdom only eight times in the Sermon on the Mount, but the Father seventeen times; and those eight times include the conclusion to the Lord's Prayer, which Jesus did not say. Someone added "for yours is the kingdom" sometime later, possibly so the church could use the prayer in public worship.

[9] Read Matt. 26:57-64, Mark 14:53-62, and Luke 22:66-71, along with John 5:18.

[10] Matt. 11:27 = Luke 10:22.

[11] Matt. 7:21; 10:32, 33; 11:27; 12:50 (2x); 18:10, 19; 20:23 (3x); 25:34; 26:29; Luke 10:22; 24:49; and numerous references in John.

[12] Gerhard Kittel takes this position in *Theological Dictionary of the New Testament*, 1: 6.

Chapter 2

Let My People Go

Jesus' metaphor of God as Abba resonated with the national, cultural memory that God had liberated his "son" Israel from Egyptian slavery in the Exodus.

When Jesus began to proclaim God as his own Father and as his audience's Father, he tapped into a deep well of rich cultural history and faith. We have to exert ourselves to grasp what the simple allusion to God as Father meant intuitively to Jesus' contemporaries. To understand that deep emotional reservoir, let's review briefly certain critically significant events in Israel's history over the twelve centuries before Jesus.

Yahweh as Israel's "Father"

Sometime in the 1200s BCE, God appeared to Moses at the burning bush in the wilderness of Sinai and called him to lead Israel out of slavery in Egypt. On that occasion Yahweh gave Moses the following instructions (author's italics):

> Then you shall say to Pharaoh, "Thus says the LORD: *Israel is my firstborn son*. I said to you, 'let *my son* go . . .'" (Exod. 4:22-23)

> Afterward Moses and Aaron went to Pharaoh and said, "Thus says the LORD, the God of Israel, 'Let *my people* go . . .'" (Exod. 5:1)

Those famous words, "Let my people go," have been robbed of much of their meaning by our ignorance of ancient Hebrew culture. Israel was God's "people" in the sense of God's family—God's "son"—even God's "firstborn son." Several centuries later, the prophet Hosea reminded Israel of that great truth revealed in the Exodus. God was Father to Israel.

> When Israel was a child, I loved him, and out of Egypt I called *my son*. (Hos. 11:1)

Here Hosea echoes God's word to Moses in Exodus 4:22-23. Hosea pointed out the family relationship between Yahweh and Israel the rest of the Hebrew Scriptures assumed. The prophet Jeremiah said the same thing in a prophecy in which "Ephraim" serves as a synonym for Israel.

> I have become a *father to Israel*, and Ephraim is *my firstborn*. (Jer. 31:9)

Yahweh "Redeemed" Israel in the Exodus

The Book of Deuteronomy said repeatedly that God had liberated his people Israel from slavery in Egypt. In the following verses, the word "redeemed" translates a Hebrew word that had come to mean metaphorically "to liberate."[1]

> For you are a people holy to the LORD your God . . . his people, his treasured possession. . . . the Lord set his heart on you and chose you . . . It was because the LORD loved you and kept the oath that he swore to your ancestors, that the LORD has brought you out with a mighty hand, and *redeemed* you from the house of slavery. (Deut. 7:6-8)

> I prayed to the LORD and said, "Lord GOD, do not destroy the people who are your very own possession, whom you *redeemed* . . . whom you *brought out of Egypt* with a mighty hand. (Deut. 9:26)

These kinds of comments about God redeeming—liberating—Israel from slavery in Egypt also appear in Deuteronomy 13:5, 15:15, 21:8, and 24:18. Not only do we see this concept in Israel's Torah, but we also read the same idea in Israel's earliest national history. That historian recorded a prayer of David as follows.

> Who is like *your people*, like Israel? Is there another nation on earth whose God went to *redeem* it as a people . . .? (2 Sam. 7:23)

The idea that Israel belongs to God as his own people whom he redeemed from Egypt also appears in the prophets.

> For I brought you up from the land of Egypt, and *redeemed* you from the house of slavery. (Mic. 6:4)

Finally, this idea of God's liberation of his people appears repeatedly in the Psalms.

> He [Yahweh] sent *redemption* to *his people*; he has commanded his covenant forever. (Ps. 111:9)

The word redeem in these occurrences had come to refer to the result of a price paid—freedom, liberation, deliverance. The concept of Israel's having been liberated held a dear place in the thinking of the Hebrew people. To call God "Father" resonated in the Jewish mind—much as July 4 and the Declaration of Independence do in American emotions.

These two themes—that Israel was God's "firstborn son" and he had redeemed and liberated them in the Exodus—became dominant in Israel's cultural memory and faith. They regularly heard these themes expounded in the Temple worship and psalms, synagogue Scripture readings, and around the family hearth. Every time they celebrated Passover, they rehearsed this history and these ideas again and again, much like an Independence Day celebration in twenty-first-century America.

God as "Father" in Jesus' Teaching

When Jesus called God "Father," he tapped into a reservoir of theology and emotion that must have moved his people mightily. They had grown up hearing that God was Israel's Father. Now they were hearing this remarkable prophet from Nazareth proclaim that the nation's Father was also their own personal Father—as individuals. Jesus did not have to spell out all these connections, for they lay in the recesses of the Jewish psyche waiting to be tapped and called into service.

When Jesus called God his Father and their Father, he also implied that God would liberate his people from all that enslaved them. To proclaim that God who had liberated Israel in the Exodus was also their own personal Father served as more than a hint that this same God was ready to liberate them from all that held them in servitude. On one occasion, though, Jesus took his metaphor of God as their Father further than on any other occasion—when he actually referred to his death as the "emancipation" by which God would set his people free. On that occasion he applied to himself a concept long held dear and central to the faith of Israelites.

Jesus as the "Liberation" of His People

A few days before his crucifixion, Jesus and his disciples hiked toward Jerusalem for the climactic events of his life. As they walked along, James and John's mother asked Jesus for a favor.[2] Recognizing Jesus as the Messiah, she also realized he would need some "right hand men" when the time came to declare himself. She asked that when he assumed his throne as Israel's messiah he give to her two sons the prime places in his kingdom's administration. In her words, she asked that he seat them at his right hand and left hand. She wanted them to be key "cabinet members" in his government.

Jesus rebuked her gently and told her she did not really understand what Messiah meant for him, that she did not know what she requested for her sons. She had unwittingly asked that they accompany him to the cross, for that was how he would enter into his reign as Messiah. Then he made possibly the most pointed statement he ever made concerning his self-sacrificial death. In that statement he paraphrased Isaiah 53:10-12 and applied it to himself.[3] Before we look at Jesus' statement, let's read Isaiah's words (with author's italics).

> Yet it was the will of the LORD to crush him with pain. When you make his *life* an *offering for sin*, he shall see his offspring, and shall prolong his days; through him the will of the LORD shall prosper. Out of his anguish he shall see light; he shall find satisfaction through his knowledge. The righteous one, *my servant*, shall *make many righteous*, and *he shall bear their iniquities*. Therefore, I will allot him a portion with the great, and he shall divide the spoil with the strong; because *he poured out himself to death*, and was numbered with the transgressors; yet he *bore the sin of many*, and made intercession for the transgressors.

Jesus boiled the entirety of Isaiah 53 and those three verses down to a single succinct sentence:

> For the Son of Man came not to be served but to serve, and to give his life a ransom for many. (Mark 10:45 = Matt. 20:28)

The Son of Man of Daniel 7:13-14 was the representative of Israel to whom God would give royal authority to reign over God's people. The Suffering Servant of Isaiah 53, on the other hand, would suffer and die as the sacrificial representative of his people. By combining the reigning Son of Man of Daniel with Yahweh's Suffering Servant of Isaiah in a conversation about messiah, he underscored that the Anointed One of Israel would not come as a conquering warrior, as many of his contemporaries envisaged. This ruler would come as a humble servant, like Isaiah's Suffering Servant. He would not come as a warrior ruler like the caesars vanquishing their enemies in their own blood. Jesus' word "serve" reflected Isaiah's words "my servant." In addition, Jesus' words "life" (Greek: *soul*) and "many" also echoed Isaiah's language.

The Greek word rendered "ransom" in most of our English translations, however, does not translate directly any specific word in the Isaiah passage. Although Isaiah 53 does not use a Hebrew equivalent of Mark's Greek word here, this word does capture Jesus' understanding of several statements in this passage that the Servant would give his life as an "offering for sin." Why, though, did Mark translate Jesus' Aramaic statement by this particular Greek word so often translated into English as "ransom"?[4] For first century Gentile Greeks, that word instantly brought to mind the manumission (emancipation, liberation) price for a slave.[5] It never, though, meant a kidnapped or captured person held for ransom in our twenty-first-century sense. For this reason, "ransom" is a poor translation of that word, a word that actually means manumission emancipation, or liberation.

We have already seen, though, that Deuteronomy (and several other places) used the word "redemption" to describe Israel's liberation from slavery in Egypt in the Exodus. Jesus' statement to the mother of James and John imported that concept—redemption—into the complex of Messiah, the Son of Man, and the Suffering Servant. Just as Yahweh, Father to Israel, had redeemed his people from slavery in the Exodus, so Jesus would give his life to liberate his people from all that enslaved them. Just as Yahweh had created his people Israel by "redeeming" them in the Exodus, so Jesus would create his own people, a new Israel, in a new Exodus, redeeming them by his sacrificial death. Jesus himself was the Father's redemption—liberation—of his people.

A Densely Packed Assertion

Before leaving this critically important statement by Jesus, we need to notice how much information Jesus packed into that short sentence. Given the context of his assertion in Mark 10:45, he merged into himself the figure of the Messiah promised by the Hebrew Scriptures, the Son of Man of Daniel 7:13-14, and the Suffering Servant of Isaiah 53. These three personages had never been combined before, as far as the record shows. On top of that triple-layered complex of ideas he piled the concept of Israel's redemption, or emancipation, from slavery in the Exodus (similar to Deut. 9:26; 2 Sam. 7:23; Mic. 6:4; Ps. 111:9). Those four ideas combined to explain the meaning of his life and self-sacrificial death on the cross awaiting at the end of that journey.

A Second Meaning of "Redemption"

This chapter has focused attention on one Hebrew word regularly translated "redeem" in the Old Testament. That word used metaphorically communicated the concept of liberation from bondage at a price. Actually, though, there are two Hebrew words in the Old Testament that translators have regularly rendered as "redeem" or "redemption." That other word and concept hold even greater significance for Jesus' teaching on what we have come to call atonement.

Notes

[1] The Hebrew word translated "redeem" here is *padah*, meaning "to liberate at a price." Since a redeemed person is thereby set free, the word came to mean simply "liberate." See *Theological Wordbook of the Old Testament*, ed. R. Laird Harris et. al. (Chicago: Moody, 1980), 2:717. This same Hebrew word stands behind the other occurrences of "redeem" in this chapter.

[2] Matt. 20:20-23.

[3] As recorded in Mark 10:43-44 and Matt. 20:28. See Donald A. Hagner, *Word Biblical Commentary: Matthew 14–28* (Dallas: Word, 1995), 582. It is nearly unanimously recognized by biblical scholars that Jesus cited Isa. 53:10-12 in this narrative.

[4] Greek: λυτρον (*lutron*).

[5] Gerhard Kittel, *Theological Dictionary of the New Testament* (Grand Rapids: Eerdmans, 1964), 4:340.

Chapter 3

Depending on Kinfolk

Jesus' metaphor of God as Abba received additional emotional resonance from Israel's faith that God was their near-kin Redeemer who had rescued them from slavery in the Exodus.

A Marital Rescue

Sometime in the 1200s BCE, the early Israelites began to settle scores of new villages in the hill country of Canaan. They were not yet the mighty nation of Israel, not having a king or an organized government of any kind. Levitical priests at Shiloh and other country shrines led the loosely knit tribes, along with occasional charismatic leaders (including one woman) they called "judges."

During this period, a famine hit Canaan.[1] A resident of Bethlehem decided it best for his family to move around the southern tip of the Dead Sea into Moab. Possibly Elimelech had heard that crops were better in Moab, so a man could support his family well there. Unfortunately, he died soon after arriving in Moab; and his wife, Naomi, found herself a widow with only her two sons, Mahlon and Chilion. In time, both sons married Moabite women. One son married a girl named Orpah, and the other a girl named Ruth. The narrative does not tell us which son married which wife. Actually, though, it does not matter; for both Mahlon and Chilion died before their wives could bear them children.

Word eventually came to Naomi that the famine in her home country had passed, crops were abundant once more, and food was readily available back in Bethlehem. She decided to return, setting out with her two daughters-in-law by her side. On the way, Naomi had misgivings about these two alien Moabites, a despised people among Hebrews, residing among Israelites and urged them to return to their own homes and marry local young men. Orpah took Naomi's suggestion and departed, but Ruth insisted on remaining with her beloved mother-in-law.

Back in Bethlehem, Naomi remembered her deceased husband had a close relative named Boaz, a wealthy farmer of advanced age. In a beautiful narrative of moving pathos, the book named for her tells how young Ruth approached Boaz and asked him to fulfill his duty as a "near kinsman." Ruth's request referred to an ancient Israelite practice similar to that of levirate marriage commanded in Deuteronomy 25:5-10. The situation described in Ruth does not follow precisely what Deuteronomy 25 commanded, but bears clear similarity to it.[2]

Levirate marriage worked as follows: If a married man died without heirs, Israelite law and custom required that his brother take his widow as wife and father children by her. In this way, three goals would be accomplished. First, the brother-in-law could protect and care for his brother's widow. Second, the dead husband's name would not die out, since the first son born of this marriage would be counted as the child of the deceased husband. Third, the husband's family would not lose their ancestral land; because the son born of this new marriage would inherit the deceased's property as his father's heir. Although not Ruth's deceased husband's brother, Boaz nevertheless filled that role by proxy.

Ruth's request overwhelmed Boaz, considering his age. He replied, though, that there was another kinsman more closely related to her departed husband than he was. We get to witness a fascinating scene of legal negotiation at the Bethlehem city gate. Boaz approached the other man and proposed that he take Ruth in levirate marriage and redeem the property of her deceased husband. The other man answered that if he did, he would endanger his own inheritance for his children. Why that should be the case is not clear from what we know of Israelite law. We only have to understand that such was the case.[3] Through concern for his own inheritance, Ruth's nearest kinsman relinquished his rights to marry her and redeem her property. (The key word in this paragraph is "redeem.")

Upon the refusal of the other man to do his duty, Boaz married Ruth, fathered a son by her, and thereby redeemed her husband's inheritance. Boaz and Ruth named that son Obed, who had a son named Jesse, who had a son named David. For the biblical narrative, this story points out that the great King David had descended from a Moabite great-grandmother—a non-Hebrew foreigner from a hated ethnic group. For us, however, the significance of this story resides in the concept of the "redeemer"—the near-kin rescuer.

Saving the Family Farm

Centuries after Ruth, Nebuchadnezzar of Babylon held Jerusalem under siege. It quickly became obvious that Judah's end lay within sight, and the nation had no future. During the siege a cousin of the prophet Jeremiah came to him, offering to sell him a family field at Anathoth. Hanamel pointed out that Jeremiah as a near kinsman had the "right of redemption" (Jer. 32:7, 8). The Hebrew word translated "redemption" came from the same root as the word translated "redeemer" in the Book of Ruth.

Ancient Hebrew law forbade the permanent removal of a family inheritance from the original owners of the property. Property must be sold to someone within the family, to someone who had the "right of redemption." In this case, "redemption" meant the rescue of the land from loss to one's family. Since Judah stood in imminent risk of destruction by the Babylonians, however, it made no sense to purchase property about to be lost entirely anyway. Nevertheless, Jeremiah bought the field from Hanamel to signal his confidence that Yahweh would protect his people and ultimately restore them to the land. In this story we have a second example of a "redeemer" rescuing his family, in this case rescuing family property from permanent loss.

The Redeemer in Ancient Israel

What many cultures hold as mere custom or emotional impulse, ancient Israel knew as a point of law. The custom had legal sanctions as well as the power of peer pressure through approbation or ostracism as enforcing powers. That institution worked in the following way.

If through poverty a woman had to sell her land to someone outside the family, her near-kin "redeemer" would re-purchase the land for her—that is, *redeem* it.[4] If a man became economically destitute, the law commanded his nearest of kin to act as his "redeemer" and rescue him by taking him into his own home. If a woman became so devastated by debt as to find it necessary to sell herself into slavery, the law commanded her next of kin to *redeem* her by purchasing her out of slavery and taking her into his family. She would not serve as his slave, however, but as his hired servant. Her servitude would last only until the year of Jubilee when she would be restored to freedom.

Ancient Hebrews used two different word-groups that both Greek and English translators have rendered as "redeem" or "redemption."[5] Only one word-group, however, included a word for "redeemer." The Hebrew word used both in the Book of Ruth and in Jeremiah meant "near-kin redeemer."[6] The concept of the near-kin redeemer, loomed large in both the ethics and theology of ancient Israel. The supreme example of the redeemer in the Old Testament lay in the concept of Yahweh as Israel's near-kin Redeemer.

Contemporary Parallels

Both legal prescriptions and social expectations circumscribed the ancient understanding of the duties of the near-kin redeemer in Israel. Peer pressure enforced those societal norms. Such a complex set of expectations seems foreign to our twenty-first-century American culture, but it is not as foreign to us as we might think. Of course, we never speak of anyone as our "redeemer," but we behave much as the ancient Israelites did.

When in trouble, we will likely call a close relative to bail us out of jail, to loan us money in a tight, or to assist us when in danger of legal disaster through debt. We assume it is our responsibility to take care of relatives who need our help, if we can. Our sense of obligation to relatives may be a sense of duty. At best, though, this loyalty to family flows from love. We cherish those nearest to us by kinship or marriage, and we want to help them if we can. Even today, we still think in many ways much as ancient Israelites did. More importantly, Jesus conceived of his calling and mission within that cultural practice and concept.

Yahweh as Israel's Near-kin Redeemer in the Exodus

When Moses returned to Egypt from the burning bush episode and demanded that the pharaoh let Israel go, the ruler responded by increasing the workload of his slaves. Moses got alone with God and poured out his heart, protesting that Israel's situation had only gotten worse since he tried to free them. God reassured Moses with affirmation and encouragement, promising Moses that he would set his people free:

> Say therefore to the Israelites, 'I am the LORD, and I will free you from the burdens of the Egyptians and deliver you from slavery to them. I will *redeem*[7] you with an outstretched arm and with mighty acts of judgment. (Exod. 6:6)

The Hebrew word translated "redeem" here means "to rescue as a near kinsman." This same word occurs in the Book of Ruth, Jeremiah, and other Old Testament passages in this sense.

As soon as Moses led Israel out of Egypt, the Pharaoh realized he had just given up his cheap work force; and he had not nearly finished his great building projects. Mounting up his crack chariot troops, he rode after his escaped slaves. Pharaoh arrived at the Red Sea too late. God had enabled the Israelites to escape through those waters; and when Pharaoh's chariots attempted to follow them, they all drowned in the same sea that had delivered the Israelites. As Moses and Israel realized the deliverance Yahweh had given them, they entered into spontaneous worship and sang a hymn of praise to Yahweh their Redeemer. In the middle of that hymn we read these words:

> In your steadfast love you led the people whom you *redeemed*; You guided them by your strength to your holy abode. (Exod. 15:13)

In one of the oldest biblical passages ever written, we see mention of God's "redeeming" his people Israel.[8] No Israelite who ever heard these words read at the temple or synagogue could forget the identity of their Redeemer. Much later in Israel's history, their hymns and prayers compiled for public worship also called God Israel's Redeemer who had come to their rescue when they were slaves in Egypt.

They remembered that God was their Rock, That God Most High was their *Redeemer*. (Ps. 78:35)

Remember your congregation, which you acquired long ago, which you *redeemed* to be the tribe of your heritage. (Ps. 74:2)

With your strong arm you *redeemed your people*, the descendants of Jacob and Joseph. (Ps. 77:15)

Jesus and his contemporaries would have heard the concept of the near-kin redeemer in the scriptural teaching in the temple and synagogue that Yahweh had redeemed them—liberated them—from Egyptian slavery. Their families inculcated that concept into them as children when they observed Passover celebrating that great occasion. They encountered near-kin redemption when they heard the Psalms read with their repeated mention of redeem, redemption, and Redeemer. Their culture reminded them constantly from childhood what that custom meant and how their faith saw God acting in their history. Jesus and his contemporaries heard the language of near-kin redemption whenever they heard the prophets read, particularly the second half of the Book of Isaiah.

A staple of Israel's theological imagery from its earliest history included the notion that Yahweh, the Israelites' Father, was therefore Israel's near-kin Redeemer who had rescued his people in the Exodus. In that great founding event, God had liberated the people of Israel from slavery in Egypt. When the Assyrians and Babylonians centuries later took them into exile, that picture of God once more shone through brilliantly, bringing them comfort and hope. They found their Redeemer still faithful in the dark night of their exile. Yahweh, who had liberated the people of Israel in the Exodus, also brought them back home in their return from exile. We now turn to examine that subject in the Book of Isaiah.

Distinguishing Jesus' Message from His Context

Jesus' good news of the loving Father stands independently of the cultural context of the near-kin redeemer. This work will offer abundant evidence in the following chapters for Jesus' message that God is our loving Father who forgives us freely, without price, without reparations. The evidence for that message is overwhelming and conclusive. Jesus clearly preached that message as his gospel.

Then as a totally separate issue, strong evidence to follow will support the significance of the words "redeem" and "redemption" in the New Testament. These words usually mean at the very least liberation, as from slavery in the Exodus. Additionally, these words frequently occur in the context of family, God as Father, believers as brothers and sisters. In other words, we commonly find the words "redeem" and "redemption" in a context consistent with near-kin redemption. If these two emphases stand independently, on the New Testament evidence, then whether we join them together as message and context becomes immaterial.

Notes

[1] We find this story in the book of Ruth.

[2] See "Excursus: The Nature of the Transaction Proposed by Boaz in vv. 3-5a" and "(2) Excursus: Levirate Marriage in the Old Testament" in Frederic Bush, *Word Biblical Commentary: Ruth/Esther* (Dallas: Word, 1996), 211-228.

[3] See the extended discussion of the complex issues involved in this scene from Ruth 4 in Bush, 229-236.

[4] These instances of prescription of redemption are delineated in Lev. 25:25-55 that legislate the responsibilities of the *go'el*, the near-kin redeemer. Deut. 25:5-10 prescribes the redemption of a man's brother's widow (or his estate) through levirate marriage. An additional example of redemption appears in Jer. 32:1-15.

[5] The verb meaning "to redeem as near kin" was *ga'al*; and the noun (actually a participle) meaning "near-kin redeemer" was *go'el*. The Septuagint (the Greek translation of the Hebrew Scriptures) translated both the *ga'al* word group and the *padah* word group (which we looked at in Chapter 2) by the λυτροω word group that we will encounter in the New Testament.

[6] In Ruth 3:9, 12 and 4:6, 14, the Hebrew noun translated "next of kin" (3:9, 12, 13; 4:1, 3, 14) and "near kinsman" (3:12) represent the Hebrew word *go'el* that comes from the same root word as the verb translated "redeem" (*ga'al*) in 4:4, 6. We encounter this same word in Job's declaration, "For I know that my Redeemer (*go'el*) lives" (Job 19:25) and in the story of Jeremiah's purchase of a field during the Babylonian siege of Jerusalem (Jer. 32:1-15), thereby "redeeming" it.

[7] The word translated "redeem" here and throughout the remainder of this chapter is *ga'al*, to redeem as a near kinsman; and the word "Redeemer" translates the Hebrew word *go'el*.

[8] See the extended discussion in John I Durham, *Word Biblical Commentary: Exodus* (Dallas: Word, 1987), 202-205. See also Ronald Hendel and Jan Joosten, *How Old is the Hebrew Bible? A Linguistic, Textual, and Historical Study* (New Haven, CT: Yale University Press, 2018), 45, 128.

Chapter 4

Redeemed from Exile

Jesus' metaphor of God as Abba also received emotional resonance from Israel's faith that God, their near-kin Redeemer, had remained faithful and redeemed them from the Babylonian Exile.

We have seen thus far that the concept of God as Father of Israel had deep roots in the faith and psyche of the nation, closely bound up as it was with their founding story of the Exodus. Yahweh had created Israel as his people when he redeemed them in the exodus from Egypt. The people of Israel saw the Exodus as God's acting as their near-kin Redeemer. Since Israel was God's "son," even God's "first-born son," he had come near to them in their Egyptian slavery as their nearest of kin to rescue them and set them free.

Those events happened sometime in the thirteenth century before Christ. Some five centuries later, Assyria took the northern nation of Israel into exile in 722 BCE, and the northern tribes of Israel ceased to exist as a nation. A century and a half later, Babylon took the southern nation of Judah into exile in 586 BCE. In Babylon, the ex-patriate Jews at first found themselves in deep depression and confusion. How could this happen to the people of God? Had God abandoned his own people?

In time, prophets arose who reassured the Jews that God had not abandoned them, that Yahweh was still their God, and they were still his people. Sometime during the Exile, a prophet arose from what historians call "the school of Isaiah"[1] to proclaim some of the most moving prophecies in the Hebrew Scriptures. We call the prophet who wrote Isaiah 40–55 Isaiah of Babylon (or Second Isaiah). After their return from Exile, another prophet of this same "school" arose, whom we call Isaiah of the Return (Third Isaiah), to write Isaiah 56–66. These two sections of the Book of Isaiah—the second half of the work—will occupy our attention for the next few pages.

The Redeemer in Isaiah of Babylon

Essentially all biblical interpreters have commented on the impact the Suffering Servant passages of Isaiah 40–55 had on Jesus' concept of the Messiah and on the New Testament as a whole. We often miss entirely, however, an equally significant point: these same passages also refer repeatedly to Yahweh as Israel's near-kin Redeemer. Isaiah of Babylon stated again and again that Yahweh who had redeemed Israel from slavery in Egypt will also redeem them from their exile in Babylon.

Abba, *Father*

The concept of the Suffering Servant of Yahweh and Yahweh as Israel's near-kin Redeemer are interwoven inseparably in these chapters.

In chapter 43, Yahweh addresses Israel as "my servant" (v. 10) and speaks tenderly to the exiled nation as his own "sons" and "daughters," proclaiming himself their near-kin Redeemer. He declares that he has forgiven their sin for no other reason than his own nature—for my own sake—and with no mention of any propitiation required to secure that forgiveness.

> But now, this is what the LORD says—he who created you, O Jacob, he who formed you, O Israel: Do not fear, for I have *redeemed*[2] you; I have called you by name, *you are mine*. . . . [B]ring *my sons* from far away and *my daughters* from the end of the earth—everyone who is called by my name, whom I created for my glory, whom I formed and made. . . . Thus says the LORD, your *Redeemer*, the Holy One of Israel, For your sake I will send to Babylon and break down all the bars, and the shouting of the Chaldeans will be turned to lamentation. . . . I, I am he who blots out your transgressions, for my own sake, and I will not remember your sins. (vv. 1, 6, 14, 25; author's italics)

In the next chapter, Yahweh as Israel's near-kin Redeemer calls on his people to return to him in repentance because of his prior redemption of them.

> Thus says the LORD, the King of Israel, and his *Redeemer*, the Lord of hosts. . . . Return to me, for I have *redeemed* you. (Isa. 44:6, 22; author's italics)

In Isaiah 45, Yahweh addresses Cyrus. In that prophecy, Yahweh calls Israel "my children" (Hebrew: "sons," v. 11). Again and again—fifteen times in sixteen chapters—we read in similar words the prophet calling Yahweh Israel's near-kin Redeemer or saying God will redeem Israel from Babylon.[3] This theme shines as brilliantly in Isaiah 40–55 as does the Suffering Servant theme. The theme of Yahweh as Israel's near-kin Redeemer usually comes in those same Suffering Servant songs.

These two motifs appear intertwined in these chapters, and we should learn to recognize them as united conceptually, like congenitally conjoined twins. Yahweh has called Israel to be his servant,[4] to be his light to the nations.[5] They are his people[6]—his sons and daughters[7]—his children.[8] Yahweh will come to them as their near-kin Redeemer[9] to save[10] them—to liberate them[11] from their bondage in the Babylonian exile. The themes of the Servant of Yahweh, liberation, Israel as Yahweh's children, and God himself as their near-kin Redeemer appear as a single complex of images throughout Isaiah 40–55.

An interesting progression takes place in the Book of Isaiah. At first, the Servant is Israel, the people of God.[12] Then the Servant morphs into a figure who calls Israel back to God.[13] And finally the Servant becomes a representative of the nation who will sacrifice himself for its people.[14] Recognizing this progression of thought illuminates Jesus' use of these passages to define his mission.

Jesus' Understanding of Messiah

On one occasion, Jesus fed five thousand people by making five barley bread cakes and two small fish go farther than any harried homemaker surprised by an unexpected visitor ever could. After that phenomenal meal, his disciples decided to go fishing. What else should they do after witnessing such an astounding miracle?

As the disciples fished during that night, Jesus walked on the water to them in the middle of the lake. When he and those commercial fishermen reached land the next day, the Lord began teaching them who he really was. In John's version of these events, he describes Jesus as saying, "And they shall all be taught by God," quoting Isaiah 54:13.[15]

We saw in the previous chapter that as Jesus moved toward Jerusalem and his crucifixion, he described his own calling by paraphrasing Isaiah 53:10-12 in a single sentence.[16] These climactic verses from the last and most striking of the Suffering Servant Songs summarized Jesus' own conception of his calling as messiah. By this point in Isaiah, the Servant of Yahweh has metamorphosed from the nation itself to a figure who will call Israel back to God and ultimately to one who will give himself sacrificially for the nation. Clearly Jesus drew his understanding of his calling as Messiah from Isaiah's Suffering Servant passages, particularly the climactic passage in 52:11–53:12.

The night before Jesus went to the cross, he led his disciples in a Passover meal we call the Last Supper. At that dinner he tried to prepare his unwary disciples for what would happen to him the next day. They would witness his crucifixion—the most horrible, excruciating, drawn-out suffering the Romans could devise. That night, one evangelist reports, Jesus cited the greatest of the Suffering Servant songs: "He was counted among the lawless" (Isa. 53:12). He went on to say, "And indeed what is written about me is being fulfilled."[17] In that simple statement he identified himself as Isaiah's Suffering Servant who would die for his people.

Most interpreters have observed the connection between the Suffering Servant passages of Isaiah and Jesus' teaching concerning himself. We should also notice as of equal importance that these same passages teach that God claims Israel as his own children, his sons and daughters, and calls himself their near-kin Redeemer.

It seems probable that when Jesus called God Father, he held all these ideas in his mind simultaneously. Just as he never found it necessary to say he was the Son of God or the Messiah, it was not necessary for him to spell out the cultural implication that God their Father was their near-kin Redeemer.

It also seems probable that the better informed members of his audiences would have seen all these connotations as implicit in Jesus' central message. His proclamation of God as their *Abba* would have resonated with historical and cultural connotations he did not need to spell out. He was proclaiming that God was not only Father of the nation but also their own dear Father as individuals. Jesus proclaimed, "God is your Father." Their memory of the Exodus, return from exile, and Yahweh as their near-kin Redeemer provided the cultural emotional context for the power of that message.

The Father Redeemer in Isaiah of the Return

Sometime after Israel had returned from exile, another prophet took up the pen to continue the work of Isaiah of Jerusalem and Isaiah of Babylon, often using their own terminology. In these chapters of the Book of Isaiah so beloved by Jesus, we continue to see many of the same emphases that appeared in Isaiah of Babylon, especially Yahweh as Israel's near-kin Redeemer. Just as Yahweh had redeemed Israel from slavery in Egypt, so he will redeem his people from exile in Babylon. The prophet envisages a time when Israel will be faithful to God, and even more, when all the nations of the world will turn to Yahweh, Israel's Redeemer. The prophet spoke of the people of God returned from exile as the children of God and of God as their Father and therefore their near-kin Redeemer.

> [A]nd you will know that I, the LORD, am Your Savior, Your *Redeemer*, the Mighty One of Jacob. (Isa. 60:16b, author's italics)

> They shall be called, "The Holy People, The *Redeemed* of the LORD"... For he said, "Surely they are *my people*, children [Heb.: sons] who will not deal falsely"; and he became their savior in all their distress. It was no messenger or angel but his presence that saved them; in his love and in his pity he *redeemed* them; he lifted them up and carried them all the days of old... For you are *our father*, though Abraham does not know us or Israel acknowledge us; you, O LORD, are *our father*, *our Redeemer* from of old is your name.... Yet, O Lord, *you are our Father*. (Isa. 62:12; 63:8-9, 16; 64:8; author's italics)

Jesus and the Book of Isaiah

Just as Jesus drew his conception of his Messiahship from Isaiah 40–55, so he interpreted his experience of God as his Father in the light of Isaiah 56–66. When Jesus cleaned out the trading tables of the money changers and animal hawkers in the Temple, he said, "It is written . . . 'My house will be called a house of prayer,'" quoting Isaiah 56:7.[18] He opened his ministry in Nazareth by preaching from Isaiah 61:1-2.[19] He cited that same passage among others when vindicating his ministry to the disciples of John the Baptist.[20] In the Sermon on the Mount, Jesus instructed his followers, "Do not swear at all: either by heaven, for it is God's throne; or by the earth, for it is his footstool."[21] There he quoted Isaiah 66:1.

On one occasion Jesus said it is better to cut off your hand or foot or gouge out your eye if it leads you into sin. (Jesus had a graphic way of making his points hyperbolically.) He went on to say, "It is better for you to enter the kingdom of God with one eye than to have two eyes and be thrown into hell [Gehenna], where 'their worm does not die, and the fire is not quenched.'"[22] That comment about the worm and fire came straight out of the last verse of the Book of Isaiah. There the prophet described a horrifying prophetic scene in which the corpses of God's enemies would be stacked up like firewood to rot and burn in the Valley of Hinnom outside Jerusalem.

Jesus regularly cited, quoted from, and preached from the second half of the Book of Isaiah. Those chapters contain all three emphases that carried Jesus' conception of his calling and message: the Suffering Servant of God, God as Father of Israel, and God as Israel's Redeemer. Jesus likely expected his hearers to recognize intuitively the rich scriptural background of his gospel. As he said several times, "He who has ears to hear, let him hear."

A Side-glance at Jeremiah

Several decades before the rise of Isaiah of Babylon, Jeremiah had preached in terms that Second and Third Isaiah (Isaiah of Babylon and Isaiah of the Return) would later elaborate. Jeremiah's prophecies were later gathered together and published in what we know as the Book of Jeremiah. The various chapters of that prophetic book were not always historically sequential, but what is important for our purpose is the book as we have it, as Jesus himself read it.

The night before his crucifixion, Jesus borrowed words from Jeremiah, words we still remember and cite often. "For the Lord has ransomed [*padah*] Jacob, and has redeemed [*ga'al*] him from the hands too strong for him" (Jer. 31:11). The word "redeemed" refers specifically to near-kin redemption; and the word translated "ransomed" often appears in the context of Israel's exodus from Egypt or return from exile. In this passage God, Father of Israel his firstborn son (v. 39), promises to bring Israel home to Jerusalem out of exile just as he once redeemed his firstborn in the exodus from Egypt. Still glancing back at the Exodus, God promises to make a new covenant with restored Israel, different from the one God made with the people of Israel after redeeming them from slavery in Egypt.

The next chapter of the Book of Jeremiah (ch. 32) contains one of the most salient examples of near-kin redemption in the Old Testament. In that chapter, Jeremiah as a near kinsman redeemed property belonging to his cousin Hanamel. The prophet went on from this act of redemption of the field to promise Judah that God would bring them back from exile and "make an everlasting covenant with them" (v. 40). Chapters 31–32 of Jeremiah are replete with allusions to near-kin redemption, exodus from Egypt, return from exile, and covenant.

The eve prior to his crucifixion, Jesus cited Jeremiah's words promising Israel a new covenant when he said at his last Passover seder, "This is my blood of the covenant which is poured out for many" (Mark 14:24). Jesus drew his words on that occasion from a passage in the center of two chapters chock full of references to near-kin redemption, exodus from slavery, return from exile, and promise of a new covenant. We probably do not read too much into Jesus' statement concerning the new covenant at his last Passover meal if we see it as implying a reference to himself as God's near-kin redemption. After all, that was the setting of his allusion in the Book of Jeremiah.

Then Why Did He Not Spell It Out?

Surely, Jesus could not have gone to these chapters in Isaiah time after time without absorbing their conception of God as Israel's near-kin Redeemer who had redeemed Israel from slavery in Egypt and from exile in Babylon. Furthermore, Isaiah was not the only prophet to use this picturesque image. Jeremiah utilized that same metaphor in the very chapter Jesus cited at the last Passover meal concerning the "new covenant" in his "blood."[23] That same chapter said Yahweh was Israel's Father, Israel was God's "firstborn son," and promised that God would redeem them from Babylon.[24] Then why did he imply his role as the Suffering Servant of Isaiah of Babylon and God as Father from both Isaiah of Babylon and Isaiah of the Return as well as Jeremiah and not teach explicitly that God was their near-kin Redeemer?

Jesus did not spell out the near-kin redemption, exodus, and return from exile connotations because those ideas did not constitute his message of what God was doing in him. Jesus preached the Good News of God as *Abba*—God as Father. Exodus from Egypt, return from exile, and near-kin Redeemer provided the cultural context that made his metaphor resonate with his original audiences. Those cultural memories and images, however, did not constitute Jesus' message. Jesus proclaimed

God as their own dear *Abba*—individually. The good news that their heavenly Father loved them and called them to fellowship with him comprised Jesus' message.

Redemption imagery provided the cultural context within which they heard Jesus' message that their loving Father called them into his fellowship. His audiences would have heard his proclamation of God as *Abba* within the cultural context of the Exodus, the return from exile, and God as their near-kin Redeemer. In the next two chapters we will see evidence that many of his hearers did draw that inference and passed it along in the oral tradition they handed on to the generations after them.

Notes

[1] See Isa. 8:16.

[2] The word translated "redeem" here and throughout the remainder of this chapter is *ga'al*, to redeem as near kin; and the word "Redeemer" translates the Hebrew word *go'el*, the near-kin redeemer.

[3] The full list consists of Isa. 41:14; 43:1, 14; 44:6, 22, 23, 24; 47:4; 48:17, 20; 49:7, 26; 52:9; 54:5, 8. In addition, 51:11 uses the word *padah* (redeem at a price).

[4] Isa. 41:8, 8; 42:2, 19; 44:1, 2, 21; 45:4; 48:17; 49:3, 5, 6.

[5] Isa. 42:6, 49:6.

[6] Isa. 40:1; 43:20; 51:4, 16, 22; 52:4, 6.

[7] Isa. 43:6.

[8] Isa. 45:11.

[9] Isa. 41:14; 43:1, 14; 44:6, 22, 23, 24; 47:4; 48:17; 48:20; 49:7, 26; 52:3, 9.

[10] Isa. 45:15, 17; 45:13; 52:7, 10.

[11] Isa. 42:7, 45:13, 49:9.

[12] Isa. 41:8; 42:18-22; 43:1, 10; 44:1-2; 49:3.

[13] Isa. 49:5-7.

[14] Isa. 50:4-8; 52:13–53:12.

[15] John 6:45.

[16] Mark 10:45.

[17] Luke 22:37.

[18] Matt. 21:13, Luke 19:46.

[19] Luke 4:14-21.

[20] Luke 7:22, Matt. 11:1-5.

[21] Matt. 5:34, 23:22.

[22] Mark 9:48.

[23] Mark 14:24 = Matt. 26:27= Luke 22:20.

[24] Jer. 31:9, 11. This verse even used both Hebrew verbs for "redeem"—first *padah* (redeem, liberate at a price) and then *ga'al* (redeem as a near kinsman). Compare Jer. 3:4 also, which calls Yahweh "Israel's Father."

Chapter 5

The Gospel According to Jesus

Jesus proclaimed that God is our loving Father who forgives our sin and calls us to trust him and live in fellowship and obedience to him.

The Four Gospels

We learned as children to recite the four New Testament gospels in sequence—Matthew, Mark, Luke, and John. It is odd, is it not, that none of them was written by the one whose name we claim as Lord and Savior. In this chapter we will review the canonical gospels' teaching as it relates to atonement and will extract from each the gospel as that author understood it, and then discern behind their various visions the gospel as Jesus himself proclaimed it.

The Gospel According to Mark

Following the death, resurrection, and ascension of Jesus, his followers began immediately to write down their remembrances of his preaching, deeds, death, and resurrection. Possibly this process began even while Jesus still walked among them. Over the years these written remembrances would have been compiled into longer collections of his teachings and deeds, filtered through the various experiences and viewpoints of individual preachers and authors.

The First Gospel

About thirty or forty years after Jesus' crucifixion and resurrection, the first Christian, as far as we know, wrote Jesus' complete story anonymously. Church tradition has given this author the name of Mark. John Mark appears in the New Testament as such a minor figure, why would anyone attribute this gospel to him if he did not write it? Whoever wrote it, he was a genius who had meditated long and lovingly on his Lord. The evidence indicates the author wrote from Rome around the time of Peter's martyrdom about 67 CE. He wrote to the suffering, persecuted believers of Rome to encourage them in their time of tribulation.

Mark gave his first hint relative to atonement in the title of his book: "The beginning of the good news of Jesus Christ, the Son of God" (1:1). In this simple title the implication of God as Father of Jesus "the Son of God" lies implicitly in the background, its significance to be revealed as the story progresses. Mark wrote as Jesus preached—inductively. He told his story simply and let the reader figure out its implications for himself. This author did not spend much time on Jesus' teaching, devoting himself primarily to what Jesus did. In his sparse reporting of Jesus' teaching, the evangelist concentrated on Jesus' proclamation of the kingdom of God. He recounted Jesus' teachings relevant to atonement only in exceedingly brief statements. We have to compare carefully what on the surface appear to be unconnected assertions to grasp Mark's understanding of Jesus' sense of his calling.

The Salvation Jesus Brought

I take the four Aramaic quotations of Jesus we looked at in Chapter 1 as Mark's own outline of his understanding of the salvation Jesus brought. (I do not mean to say these quotations constitute the outline of the book but merely the outline of Mark's understanding of Jesus' good news.) In the story of the raising of Jairus' daughter, Jesus' Aramaic command *Talitha koum* ("Little girl, arise," 5:41) served as more than a story that Jesus raised an adolescent girl from the dead. That quotation indicated Mark's conviction that Jesus came to liberate humanity from death. This story hinted at Jesus' own resurrection to come. Possibly it also threw a backward glance at Ezekiel's vision of the valley of dry bones (Ezek. 37:1-14) and Israel's promised "resurrection" in return from exile.

When Jesus healed the deaf mute with the Aramaic imperative *Ephphatha* ("Be opened"), Mark commented, "[H]is ears were opened, his tongue was *released*" (Mark 7:34-35). This vignette meant more than that Jesus performed a miracle in healing a deaf mute. Mark intended us to understand that Jesus came to open our ears to God—even to open *us* to God—and to release us from all that holds us in bondage. The word translated "released"[1] meant "set free." The second point of Mark's understanding of Jesus' gospel was deliverance from all that binds us. Possibly this story contained a subtle backward look at Israel's release in its redemption from Egypt and later from Exile.

Climactically, as Jesus prayed in Gethsemane in anticipation of his crucifixion the next day, Mark tells us Jesus prayed in Aramaic, *Abba*. That single agonized cry encapsulated the meaning of Jesus' life and message. He lived in awareness of God as his Father and taught that God is our Father, too.

The next day Jesus cried out from the cross, *Eloi, Eloi, lema sabachthani* ("My God, my God, why have you forsaken me?" 15:34). With that final Aramaic quotation, Mark told us that in order to bring us back to God our Father and thereby liberate us from death and all that binds us, Jesus descended into the lowest pit of human experience. He joined us—he took our place—in our deepest feeling of abandonment by God.

The Gospel According to Jesus

Jesus' New Family

Interspersed within this Aramaic outline of his vision of the meaning of Jesus' life, message, death, and resurrection, the evangelist provided other significant narratives that tip us off to his conception of the meaning of this remarkable man. When Jesus' family came to take him home as a hopeless madman, Jesus told the assembled crowd that his true family consisted of "whoever does the will of God" (3:21, 31-35).

When Peter pointed out that the Twelve had left everything to follow Jesus, he replied: "There is no one who has left house or brothers or sisters or mother or father or children or fields, for my sake and for the sake of the good news, who will not receive a hundredfold now in this age—houses, brothers and sisters, mothers and children, and fields, with persecutions—and in the age to come eternal life" (10:29-30). With these two brief stories, Mark told us Jesus had come to call us to a new family—the family of God—in time and eternity. These two narratives take on profound meaning when combined with Mark's climactic point that Jesus knew God as his *Abba*.

Though untutored in proper Greek, Mark's gospel demonstrates that he had mastered the art of rhetoric. As one of his favored devices, he taught by surprise. We observe an example of this practice in that, although he taught Jesus' new family from early in his gospel, he seldom quoted Jesus as calling God his Father. Prior to the end of this original gospel, Mark depicted Jesus as referring to God as Father only three times, all in the second half of his narrative.[2] By limiting his citations of Jesus calling God his Father until the second half and the climax of his narrative, Mark set his readers up to be startled by observing Jesus at prayer crying out to God as his own personal Father—his *Abba*.

Liberation for Many

In Chapter 2 we examined the highly significant vignette when the mother of James and John asked that her sons be given preferred appointments in Jesus' kingdom. On that occasion Mark set forth Jesus' one explicit statement regarding his self-sacrificial death. Jesus' response to the solicitous mother identified himself as the Suffering Servant prophesied by Isaiah who would give himself sacrificially for the liberation of his people.[3] He referred to himself as the "emancipation for many" (contemporary translations usually render the key word here "ransom"), meaning God's liberation or redemption for many, parallel to God's redemption of Israel in the Exodus. In this statement Jesus packed a lot into a few words. A few days later, as Jesus celebrated Passover with his disciples, he told them that the cup of wine they drank "is my blood of the covenant which is poured out for many" (Mark 14:24).[4] Those words echoed his statement to James and John's mother that he would give his life as an "emancipation," a redemption, for many.[5]

Son of God

Later that night at his trial, Jesus uttered his second densely worded assertion of his identity. He replied to the high priest's interrogation that he was indeed the Christ, the "Son of the Blessed One"; "and you will see the Son of Man sitting at the right hand of the Mighty One and coming on the clouds of heaven" (14:62). In that cross-examination Jesus finally asserted that he was the Messiah, the Son of God. That affirmation sealed his conviction for blasphemy and condemnation to death. To make sure his readers did not miss his point, Mark reported that the centurion in charge of his grisly crucifixion said, "Truly this man was God's Son!" (15:39). The first evangelist ended his gospel as he had begun it: "with Jesus Christ, the Son of God."

In his own understated style, Mark saved most of his hints of Jesus' understanding of his atonement for the last few days and even the last twenty-four hours prior to his burial. Even in those powerful, pithy statements, though, Mark left it to his readers to grasp inductively the meaning of Jesus' life and death. The Good News for Mark is that the Father *Abba* has sent his Son to rescue us, to free us, holding nothing back in the process. In the end, Jesus sacrificed himself to liberate—to redeem—us from death and all that binds us; to call us back to our Father; to establish in his own blood the Father's new covenant written on our hearts. Our Father-Redeemer pursued us all the way to the cross to bring us back into fellowship with himself and calls us to take up our cross and live as Jesus did.

The Message of the Gospels

GOSPEL	DATE	RELEVANT FEATURES
Mark	ca. 67	• Begins with Jesus the Son of God (1:1) • Major emphasis: the kingdom of God • Jesus' new family (3:31-35, 10:29-30) • Liberation from all that binds (5:41, 7:34) • Suffering Servant of Isaiah (10:45) • Redemption for many (10:45) • The new covenant (14:24) • Prayer to Abba (14:36) • Messiah & Son of God (14:62) • Depths of human experience (15:34) • Concludes with Jesus Son of God (15:39)

GOSPEL	DATE	RELEVANT FEATURES
Matthew	ca. 80–85	• Organization implies Jesus is the new Moses • Jesus and the new Exodus (2:15) • Major emphasis: the kingdom of heaven • Greater emphasis on the Father than in Mark • Focus on the Father's kingdom (5–7) • Jesus' new family (12:50, 19:29) • The kingdom of the Father (13:43) • Redemption for many (20:28) • "My Father's kingdom" at end (26:29) • Prays to his Father (26:39-42)
Luke	ca. 80–85	• "Redemption" at the beginning (1:68, 2:38) • Major emphasis: the kingdom of God • Greater emphasis on the Father than in Mark • Jesus calls God "my Father" (2:49) • The Father's new family (8:21, 18:29) • Jesus' crucifixion & resurrection his "Exodus" (9:31) • The kingdom from the Father (12:32) • Central Parable: Prodigal Son (15:11-32) • "Redemption" at the end (21:28, 24:21) • Commends his spirit to the Father (23:46) • Promise of the Spirit from the Father (24:49)
John	ca. 90	• Major emphasis: the Father • Lesser emphasis: eternal life rather than the Kingdom • Reunion with the Father promised (14:1-6) • Prayer to his Father (17:1-26) • Speaking of his Father (20:17, 21)

The Gospel According to Matthew

A decade or so after Mark wrote his gospel, another anonymous Jewish believer, probably in Syria, wrote a gospel to instruct Jews recently converted to faith in Jesus. We have no idea who this author was, but let's call him by his traditional name. Matthew began with Mark's gospel as the scaffolding of his good news, incorporating most of that first gospel into his own. To that original gospel he added material gathered from a variety of sources, probably both oral traditions and written accounts of those traditions.

The New Moses

Like Mark, Matthew told of Jesus' deeds. This evangelist, however, also gave a great deal of attention to Jesus' teachings, mostly derived from the other traditions available to him. He alternated his narratives of Jesus' deeds with Jesus' teachings throughout his gospel. Matthew organized his gospel into five sections, parallel to the five "books of Moses" of the Pentateuch (Genesis through Deuteronomy). In this way he showed the parallel between Jesus' mission and Moses' leading Israel out of Egyptian slavery in the Exodus. Matthew even emphasized this connection at the beginning of his narrative by quoting Hosea's statement, "Out of Egypt I have called my son" (2:15, quoting Hos. 11:1). Hosea spoke this of Yahweh's redemption of Israel from slavery in Egypt. Matthew applied Hosea's statement to Jesus as the redemption of his people in a new Exodus.

The Good News of the Father

Matthew described Jesus' teaching concerning the kingdom far more often than did Mark. At the same time, he reported that Jesus spoke of the Father almost as often as of the kingdom. He actually tied the theme of the Father to that of the kingdom in numerous stories.[6] Matthew made it clear that he understood the kingdom to belong to the Father. Jesus' kingdom was headed by his loving Father, not by a political monarch. Whereas Mark had depicted Jesus as calling God "Father" or *Abba* only four times, Matthew multiplied that pattern many times over.

Significantly, Matthew placed Jesus' Sermon on the Mount near the beginning of his gospel, apparently signaling by this placement that this sermon provides the theme of Matthew's understanding of the Good News Jesus preached.[7] In this collection of Jesus' teachings, as he proclaims the coming of the kingdom he speaks of the Father more than twice as often as of the kingdom. Whereas in Mark, Jesus proclaimed the Good News of the kingdom, in Matthew, Jesus proclaimed the Good News of the Father's kingdom. Jesus taught his disciples to pray to their loving heavenly Father, confident that he will give them good things even as their earthly fathers have done. His followers are to forgive, love, and bless in imitation of their heavenly Father. They are to perform their religious acts as to their Father and not for the eyes of others.

The Father's New Family

Matthew shared Mark's viewpoint that Jesus called his followers to enter a new family—of believers. He repeated the story he received from Mark's gospel of Jesus' family coming to see him. (Possibly discounting as irreverent Mark's assertion that they thought Jesus mad, Matthew left that comment out of his account.) Like Mark, Matthew reported that Jesus asserted on that occasion that his family consisted of "whoever does the will of my Father in heaven" (12:49).

Matthew also copied Mark's story of Peter saying the disciples had forsaken everything to follow Jesus. To this claim, Jesus replied that those who had left family behind to follow him would receive a new family "a hundredfold, and will inherit eternal life" (19:29). He reported that Jesus said "you have one Father" (23:9) and that they were all brothers and sisters of one another. Through these sayings of Jesus, we come to understand the kingdom as the family of God.

Matthew, too, explained the teachings and deeds of Jesus as fulfilling the promise of Isaiah concerning the Suffering Servant of the Lord. Then Matthew went on to describe Jesus as teaching that he had come to liberate—to redeem—God's people from bondage to sin and death as God had redeemed Israel from slavery in Egypt so long ago.[8]

It's All about the Father

In a powerful chapter Matthew quoted Jesus as saying, "You have one Father—the one in heaven" (23:9). Almost immediately after that reassuring word, Jesus rebuked the religious leaders for giving exquisite attention to worship rituals and legal niceties while neglecting "the more important matters of the law: justice, mercy, and faithfulness" (v. 23, NIV). The implication sounds through clearly—your Father cares more about faithfulness to his revealed character and will than for legalistic rules. Jesus came to effect a new relationship with the Father, not to fulfill a legal requirement of a heavenly Judge.

Throughout this gospel the evangelist described Jesus' teaching concerning the Father in highly personal terms.[9] Take the Lord's Prayer as an example. Matthew's insertion of the possessive pronoun "our" captures Jesus' tender personal way of addressing his Father. Every source we have for the life of Jesus depicts him as speaking of God as his own Father.[10] Matthew's gospel has been described as the Good News of the kingdom; it is also the Good News of the Father. The Jews had always known God as the Father of Israel; but Jesus announced that God was his personal Father, in addition to the Jews' heavenly Father.

On the night before his crucifixion, Jesus observed Passover with his disciples. As he established his new covenant with a glass of wine, he said, "I will never again drink of this fruit of the vine until that day when I drink it new with you in my Father's kingdom" (26:29). Among the last words he spoke to his disciples before his death, he climactically joined the concept of God as their Father with the kingdom he was establishing. Again, like Mark, Matthew wrapped up the message of Jesus in the Good News of the loving Father. Stephen Finlan points out that Jesus' proclamation of the kingdom embodies an oddity—a kingdom, but no king.[11] This kingdom is headed by the Father, not a king. Jesus truly preached a kingdom like no other. For Jesus, the kingdom of God was the family of God.

The Gospel According to Luke

About the same time Matthew wrote his gospel, Luke wrote his (around 80–85 CE). It seems likely that Paul's companion, Luke, wrote this gospel. As with Mark, why would anyone attribute a gospel to such a forgettable New Testament character as Luke unless he actually wrote it? Like Matthew, Luke used Mark's gospel as the spine of his gospel, adding to it material he derived from sources such as oral traditions and written records of oral traditions.[12]

Jesus, God's Redemption

Mark's gospel exposed to our view Jesus' unique practice of calling God *Abba*. Matthew's gospel gave even greater attention to Jesus teaching tenderly of his Father. Luke carries us a step further by seeing the significance of Jesus in the concept of redemption. In the first chapter of his gospel Luke described the father of John the Baptist as proclaiming that God was coming to make "redemption" for "his people."[13]

The significance of that word resides in the fact that this Greek word-group[14] had been used by the ancient translators of the Hebrew Scriptures into Greek to render both Hebrew words for redemption.[15] In this usage, Luke cast an implicit look backward to the Israelites' exodus from Egypt and to their return from the Babylonian Exile. This word would even have suggested to the well informed among them the connotation of near-kin redemption.

The word redemption here clearly means at the very least deliverance, or liberation.[16] The mention of God's "people,"[17] however, suggests that Luke also intended to hint at God as Israel's near-kin Redeemer, as in the Hebrew Scriptures. The mention of the "tender mercy of our God" (1:78) provides a further indication of Luke's conception of the nature of the salvation, the redemption, provided in Jesus. Atonement is reconciliation to our loving Father, not placation of an angry deity. Luke quickly followed up that narrative by describing old Anna at the Temple at the infant Jesus' dedication as looking for the redemption—the liberation—of Jerusalem.[18] Luke's understanding of the salvation brought by Jesus included first of all deliverance, liberation, of God's people.

We receive the conclusive indication of Luke's conception of the "redemption" Jesus proclaims and embodies in his narrative of the Transfiguration. Mark and Matthew said only that Moses and Elijah appeared "talking with Jesus" (Mark 9:4, Matt. 17:3). Luke, however, added to Mark's narrative that they were discussing with Jesus his "Exodus" (*exodon* in Greek, Luke 9:31). Several authors of the Hebrew Scriptures, as we have already seen, had described the Exodus as God's redemption of Israel. This single word in this highly significant story provides the critically important hint to the precise importance of Luke's word redemption. In Jesus' upcoming crucifixion and resurrection, like Moses, he would lead his people in Exodus, providing them with redemption.

Luke saw God's redemption, furthermore, as given to all people; not just to the Jews. He gave more attention than any other evangelist to Jesus' love for Gentiles as well as neglected and marginalized people—women, the poor, "sinners" (those not meticulously keeping Judaism's traditional rules), foreigners, traitorous publicans, and untouchable lepers. He described Jesus as having women disciples[19] who traveled with him. Jesus even made a member of a despised ethnic group the hero of his parable of the good Samaritan.[20]

The Loving Father

Like Mark, Luke highlighted the kingdom of God as Jesus' major emphasis; but he gave greater attention than Mark to Jesus' proclamation of the good news of the loving Father. He did not emphasize the Father as much as Matthew did, but still that emphasis shines through if we pay attention. The following passages illustrate this point.

Early in his gospel he quoted the boy Jesus as saying he must be in his "Father's house" (2:49). Like Matthew, Luke included in his narrative Mark's story of Jesus saying that his "mother and brothers" were "those who hear the word of God and do it" (8:21). Jesus not only related to God as his personal Father[21], but he also called around him a new family and taught them to see God as their own Father.[22] He taught his disciples not to worry about providing for their needs, but to trust their Father who knows all and will provide for them.[23] In the middle of the third gospel, Luke quoted Jesus as saying, "Do not be afraid, little flock, for it is your Father's good pleasure to give you the kingdom" (12:32). The kingdom of God is the kingdom ruled by the loving Father—that is, the family of God.

Luke's crowning account of Jesus' Good News came in his narrative of the prodigal son.[24] In this story the younger son wastes his father's fortune in wild living. When he returns home broke and broken, the father welcomes the lost son back into his arms and throws a party. In this simple illustration we learn Jesus' definition of atonement—reconciliation with the Father. The only requirements are the son's repentance, the Father's joyful forgiveness, and the estranged son's acceptance of it.

Concluding as He Began

As Luke draws toward the end of his gospel narrative, he returns to his theme of redemption with which he had begun. During the last week before Jesus' crucifixion, Luke quoted Jesus as saying, "When these things begin to take place, stand up and raise your heads, because your redemption is drawing near" (21:28).

Following Jesus' resurrection, he appeared to a couple on the road to Emmaus. In that conversation, one of the two said concerning their grief at Jesus' crucifixion, "But we had hoped that he was the one to redeem Israel" (24:21). Luke ended his gospel as he had begun it—with Jesus proclaimed as the redemption of both Israel and all humankind sent by the Father. As Moses led Israel in the exodus from Egypt, Jesus would lead his followers in a new exodus from bondage into full freedom.

Toward the end of his book, at the Last Supper, Luke quoted Jesus again as combining the themes of the kingdom and the Father: "I confer on you, just as my Father has conferred on me, a kingdom, so that you may eat and drink at my table in my kingdom" (22:29-30). Mark, Matthew, and Luke in different ways all climaxed their stories of Jesus by pointing out that Jesus' good news centered on the kingdom ruled by his loving Father.

The Gospel According to John

A decade or so after Matthew and Luke (ca. 90 CE), another anonymous disciple in the vicinity of Ephesus wrote the fourth gospel. He seems to have been a Jew of Greek culture, basing his gospel either on the testimony of the Apostle John or on that of some other notable "beloved disciple" of Jesus. He wrote a series of meditations built around the stories John had remembered and taught his disciples. In his presentation of Jesus he reinterpreted and restated the Good News for a Greek cultural setting. His own thoughts so intruded into his narrative, however, that we find it difficult to separate John's thoughts from those of Jesus. At any rate, the Fourth Gospel tells us how this believer at the end of the first century understood the significance of Jesus.

Gospel of Eternal Life

This Hellenistic disciple replaced the earlier gospels' emphasis on the kingdom of God with that of eternal life. Even so, he gave evidence that he knew of Jesus' preaching of the kingdom. Early in his gospel John told of Jesus talking to Nicodemus about seeing and entering the kingdom.[25] Then at the end of his narrative he described Jesus speaking to Pilate about his kindom.[26] By bracketing his gospel of eternal life in this way, he signaled that he knew precisely what he was doing: he was redefining what Jesus meant by the kingdom of God. The kingdom signified intimate communion with the Father for time and eternity.

By "eternal life," John did not mean just life in heaven forever, but God's quality of life.[27] He created metaphor after metaphor to describe what God was doing in Jesus. Through all the varied pictures, though, the central truth came shining through: the Father has come in his Son to enable us to share God's quality of life—now and forever.

While John's gospel has been called the gospel of eternal life, it refers to the Father three times as often as to eternal life.[28] John heard Jesus' emphasis on the Father sounding down through the decades. The hint that arose in Mark's gospel, rose in volume in Matthew's, developed into explicit reference to "redemption" in Luke's, swelled to full crescendo loudly proclaiming the Father in John's. Clearly the early church remembered Jesus' proclamation of the Father more powerfully than anything else he preached. John brought his linkage of the Father, the Son, and eternal life[29] to its climactic statement in Jesus' prayer at the end of Jesus' last Paschal meal:

> Father, the hour has come; glorify your Son so that the Son may glorify you. . . . And this is eternal life, that they may know you, the only true God, and Jesus Christ whom you have sent. (17:1, 3)

In My Father's House

At that Last Supper, Jesus prepared his disciples for the ordeal awaiting them the next day and for the rest of their lives. He told them that in the compound of "my Father's house" there are many homes. Like a first-century Jewish son preparing to bring his bride home, Jesus would prepare a place for his bride near the Father. Then he would take his bride home to enjoy his presence in the light of the Father's face in *Abba's* house. He clinched that story by saying, "I am the way, and the truth, and the life. No one comes to the Father except through me" (14:6).

In that brief parable, as in Jesus' prayer, lies John's conception of the atonement Jesus provided—reconciliation with our Father through the Son. Significantly, all four gospels bring Jesus' gospel of the loving Father to its climax on his last night before he gave his life for us all. Can we doubt that the Father's love, the Father's family, the Father's house constituted the central theme of Jesus' thought and preaching?

Also at the Last Supper, Jesus told his disciples exactly how their lives would be transformed.[30] He told them that "the Holy Spirit whom the Father will send in my name" would transform their lives (14:26).

The Gospel According to Jesus

What these varying portrayals of Jesus of Nazareth hold in common reveals the gospel and atonement according to Jesus as our oldest accounts proclaimed him. At the risk of oversimplifying, the following paragraphs summarize Jesus' Good News in its simplest form. Of course, his preaching and teaching included far more than the points delineated below, but here is a distillation of the gospel according to Jesus—the Good News he proclaimed and to which he called his fellow Jews and all who would accept his message.

Abba, *Father*

Call to the Father's Family

Jesus preached that the kingdom is the Father's kingdom—our loving Father's rule over us. Our Father reigns over us, loves us, forgives us, calls us, waits for us, and throws a party to welcome his wayward children home. Marcus Borg has written that the kingdom for Jesus represented "what life would be like on earth if God were king and the rulers of this world were not."[31] Since our Lord represented the kingdom as ruled by the Father, we could also say that for Jesus the kingdom means what life is like on earth when we function as our Father's family instead of as politico-economic power systems.

Then with his children reconciled to himself, the Father begins to heal the damage we have done to ourselves through our rebellion by his own presence in his Spirit. Having begun his healing process, he works through us by his Spirit to heal our society of the damage done by our ignorant and deliberately evil deeds. Our Father will leave nothing undone in his work of liberation, until we are all ushered into the final consummation of that reconciliation, gathered around the Father—"in my Father's house."

Jesus did not present a theory of the atonement—a literal, legal explanation of how his death enabled God to forgive us. He preached a metaphor of atonement—the emotionally moving metaphor of God as our Father forgiving his prodigal children and drawing us to himself. That metaphor drew its attractive power in the first century from the cultural metaphor of God as Israel's near-kin Redeemer coming to rescue and free his people from bondage, whether from slavery in Egypt or from exile in Babylon.

A metaphor, however, is never just a metaphor. It always points to something. Whatever the metaphor signifies is the truth proclaimed. Jesus' metaphor of the loving Father drawing near to reconcile us to himself points to an *explanation* of atonement—God loves us and calls us into his fellowship. The God and Father of the Lord Jesus Christ only asks for our repentance (turning away from rebellion and self-will) and acceptance (faith) of the reconciliation (atonement) with him he so joyfully offers. Atonement is not about explaining how the cross of Christ saves us; it is our heavenly Father reconciling us to himself through Jesus.

All the Way to the Cross

Of course, Jesus' explanation of atonement included the cross—it required it. He had to go to the cross in order to pursue God's lost children all the way. It cost him everything. He paid the price, as we say of soldiers who die in combat for their fellow soldiers and their nation. As Fisher Humphreys argued decades ago, the Gospels present atonement in Jesus Christ as "cruciform forgiveness"—God's atonement of his alienated children to himself shaped by Jesus' self-sacrificial death on the cross. God embodied his character and nature in Jesus of Nazareth. In his teaching, life, and death, Jesus revealed our loving Father who pursues us to the point of total identification with us in death on the cross. The Father of grace came to us in Jesus of Nazareth, calling us back to himself; identifying himself with us in hunger and thirst, pain and fatigue, and ultimately in an ignominious death.

Like a stoned addict lying in a back alley, when our loving Father bent over to rescue us in Jesus, in our confusion and even rebellion, we lashed out and murdered him. Then the Father vindicated everything his Son had claimed and implied about himself and his Father by resurrecting him from the dead. Having done everything possible to call us back to himself, having allowed his rebellious children to kill his embodiment in his Son, he forgives us and calls us to reconcile with himself. He requires nothing more.

The cross of Jesus sealed his witness to the Father. His submission to crucifixion expressed and bestowed his Father's grace and forgiveness in the most radical way possible. His resurrection constituted his Father's affirmation of that witness, life, and death. His resurrection also enthroned the risen Christ as Lord of the church and of the cosmos. His atonement, however, did not lie in his death alone. Atonement—reconciliation—flowed from the entirety of his witness to the Father in his life, teaching, death, and resurrection.

Impact on Jesus' Earliest Disciples

It seems reasonable that Jesus' proclamation of the Good News of the Father's love and forgiveness would have resonated among Jesus' earliest disciples with overtones of near-kin redemption. If this book is correct in its understanding of Jesus' Good News and the cultural context that gave it emotive power, then we should see both those themes echoed in the preaching and teaching of the first-century church. Do we? The next chapter will explore the way the first-century church proclaimed the gospel of Jesus Christ.

Notes

[1] Greek: λυω (*luo*), to set free.
[2] Mark 8:38, 11:25, 13:32.
[3] Isa. 53:12.
[4] Jer. 31:31-34.
[5] Possibly we can even see in these two statements taken together an implicit reference to Psalm 111:9: "He [Yahweh] sent redemption [Heb: *peduth*; Grk: λυτρωσιν] to his people; he has commanded his covenant forever," where the psalmist combined redemption with covenant.
[6] Matt. 6:32-33, 7:21, 13:43, 18:35, 20:23, 23:9, 25:34, 26:29.

[7] The following material comes from Matthew 5–7.

[8] Matt. 22:28, paraphrasing Isa. 53:10-12.

[9] He did so 45 times, attaching a possessive personal pronoun to the word "Father" in all but three cases. He called God "my Father" 17 times and "your Father" 18 times. Although that usage appears in all the gospels, only in Matthew is it the almost universal pattern.

[10] Twice when Matthew quoted Jesus as referring to God as Father, he derived the quotations from Mark (Matt. 16:27 = Mark 8:38; Matt. 6:14 = Mark 11:25.) Six times he gleaned his quotations from that document scholars call "Q," which probably dates to the 50s CE (Matt. 5:45, 48; 6:9, 26, 32; 7:11.) The other 34 times his quotations came from his own unique sources (designated "M" by scholars). This tells us that Matthew knew at least three different lines of tradition (Mark, Q, and M) that reported Jesus knew God as his own Father and taught that God is our own Father.

[11] Stephen Finlan, *The Family Metaphor in Jesus' Teaching: Gospel Imagery and Application*, 2nd ed. (Eugene, OR: Cascade, 2013), 82.

[12] Conventionally called "L," a fourth source where Jesus taught that God was his Father.

[13] Luke 1:68.

[14] The λυτροω (*lutroo*) family of words.

[15] Both the Hebrew word *padah* (as discussed in chapter 2) and *ga'al/go'el* (as discussed in chapters 3 and 4).

[16] Compare the words "rescued from our enemies" in v. 73.

[17] See the mention of "his people" also in v. 77.

[18] Luke 2:38.

[19] Luke 8:1-3.

[20] Luke 10:25-37.

[21] See Jesus' startling statement in Luke 10:21-22.

[22] Luke 11:13.

[23] Luke 12:30.

[24] Luke 15:11-32.

[25] John 3:3, 5.

[26] John 18:36.

[27] I owe this wording of the meaning of "eternal life" to Greek and New Testament professor at New Orleans Baptist Theological Seminary, Dr. Ray Robbins.

[28] John spoke of "life" or "eternal life" 37 times; he referred to "the Father" 115 times.

[29] John 5:19-26, 6:27-47, 17:3.

[30] John 14–16.

[31] Marcus Borg, *The Heart of Christianity: Rediscovering a Life of Faith* (New York: HarperOne), 132.

Chapter 6

The First-century Church

Apart from Jesus' teaching, the New Testament follows Jesus in depicting God most often as Father; at times, it also reflects awareness of the implication that Jesus, the Father's near-kin redemption, recalled Israel's redemption in the Exodus and return from exile.

If the case argued so far is correct, then we should see certain key points echoed in the earliest writings of the Christian church—both by explicit statement and by omission. The New Testament should reflect the views of the earliest church in three distinct traits. First, we should see an absence of description of salvation by propitiation. Second, New Testament authors following the Gospels should constantly repeat Jesus' metaphor of the Father. Third, we should find at least occasional references to "redemption" in language that recalls Israel's liberation from slavery in Egypt and even implying near-kin redemption.

We have observed already that all the first-century gospels did describe Jesus as teaching about his Father. Luke, for example, implied five times that Jesus' mission paralleled Israel's redemption in the Exodus. Even Mark and Matthew both quoted Jesus himself as using redemption language on one occasion to describe his mission. Now we move on to examine how the first century church viewed and taught the meaning of Jesus of Nazareth as evidenced in the Book of Acts, the Epistles, and the Book of Revelation.

Abandoning the Jewish Concept of Propitiation

The first-century church had two sets of Scriptures: the Hebrew Scriptures and its Greek translation, the Septuagint (LXX). A comparison of the Greek New Testament with the Septuagint yields a startling finding: the first-century church as reflected in the New Testament rejected the concept of propitiation in which they had been reared. The Jews had a full vocabulary of Greek words to express their idea of propitiation—that we must placate God with sacrifices before he will forgive. The most distinctive of those words never appear in the New Testament.

Even though the Jews read the Greek Septuagint as Scripture, they rarely employed any of its distinctive words for propitiation to describe Jesus' death.[1] The writings of the first-century church that have survived until today never used any of the four most popular words for propitiation in the Septuagint to describe the death of

Christ as appeasing God.² Even the two minor Septuagint terms from this vocabulary appear only four times.³ Even then, those two words did not mean propitiation.⁴ One other word translated "propitiation" in the King James Version—but not in most other contemporary translations—never appears in the Septuagint with that meaning.⁵

Many statements in the Old Testament either said or could be taken as meaning that God must be appeased, placated, "propitiated," before he will forgive. The New Testament authors refrained from using the four words teaching that theology—favorite words in their own Greek Scriptures! Because of the teaching, life, death, and resurrection of Jesus, the first-century church rejected the concept of propitiation taught by the Hebrew Scriptures. The early Christians not only did not use the distinctive vocabulary that described such appeasement of God, but they also did not communicate the concepts. (See "Propitiation in the Septuagint and New Testament" below.)

Paul, for example, did speak of the "wrath of God," but in Romans 1:18-31 he spiritualized that concept to mean that God allows us to experience the natural results of our failure to live according to God's will. It seems early Christian leaders tried to make sure no one misunderstood them to teach that Jesus' death in any way paid some debt that God required before he would forgive.

If Christians in the first century rejected the standard Old Testament concept of propitiation, then how did they teach that God has saved us through Jesus Christ? They created metaphor after metaphor to illustrate the salvation God offers us through his Son. (See "Varied New Testament Metaphors of Salvation," p. 56, for a partial list of those metaphors with representative texts using them.) Not once, though, did they attempt to construct a literal, legal explanation of how the cross of Christ made it possible for God to forgive and save us. Of the more than twenty metaphors used by the first-century church as recorded in the New Testament, only one found universal usage: Father. A second, sacrifice, achieved near universal popularity. The third most popular metaphor, redemption, appears in the work of several different writers.

Propitiation in the Septuagint and the New Testament

GREEK	MEANING	HEBREW	LXX	NT
ἐξιλασκομαι/ exilaskomai	propitiate	kaphar⁶	83 times, including Lev. 9:7	---
"	expiate, forgive	"	4 times, including 2 Chron. 30:18	---

The First-century Church

GREEK	MEANING	HEBREW	LXX	NT
ἐξιλασμος/ exilasmos	atonement	kapporeth	1 Chron. 28:11	---
"	"	kippurim	Exod. 30:10; Lev. 23:27, 28	---
"	propitiation	chatte	Ezek. 43:23	---
ἐξιλασις/ exilasis	"	chattath	Num. 29:11	---
ἐξιλασμα/ exilasma	bribe, ransom	kopher	1 Sam. 12:3, Ps. 48:8	---
ἱλασκομαι/ hilaskomai	repent, be sorry	naham	Exod. 32:14	---
"	be merciful, forgive	salak	2 Kgs. 5:18, 24:4; Lam. 3:42	Luke 18:13
"	forgive, cover	kaphar	Ps. 65:3, 78:38, 79:9	Heb. 2:17
ἱλασμος/ hilasmos	restitution, propitiation	"	Num. 5:8	---
"	forgive, forgiveness	salach selichah	2 Kgs. 5:18; 2 Chron. 6:30; Ps. 24:11, 129:4	---
"	forgive	kaphar	Ps. 77:38, 79:9	---
"	atonement	kippurim	Lev. 25:9, Ezek. 44:27	1 John 2:2, 4:10 possibly
"	sin offering	ashemah	Amos 8:14	1 John 2:2, 4:10 probably
ἱλαστηριον/ hilasterion[7]	mercy seat	kaporeth	21 times, including Exod. 25:17	Rom. 3:25, Heb. 9:5
"	capital	kaphtor	Amos 9:1	---
"	altar ledge	azarah	Ezek. 43:14, 17, 20	---

Father

The first-century church heard Jesus loud and clear in his constant reference to God as his and our Father. Even a cursory examination of the New Testament shows first-century authors called God "Father" more than twice as often as they used any other metaphor.[8] The predominance of the Father metaphor seems highly significant. The letters attributed to Paul repeatedly call God "the Father."[9] Of course, Jews had long thought of God as Father of the people of Israel; but Acts, the Epistles, and the Revelation contain a different thrust. These writers also spoke of God as their own personal Father. Clearly, they learned this concept from Jesus and adhered to it in faithfulness to his teaching.

Admittedly, the New Testament does not state an explicit explanation of atonement in terms of God's Fatherhood. But then, it does not state any explicit doctrine of atonement at all. Jesus' emphasis on the Fatherhood of God, however, had so impressed itself on the minds of his disciples that they could not write of their faith and salvation without referring repeatedly to that great revealed truth. Only the exceedingly short personal note in 3 John lacks such a mention, and even that writer had already called God "Father" four times in 2 John.

We may find it easy to miss the significance of the frequent New Testament allusions to God as Father, because many of those references seem so casual. For instance, when letter writers open their epistles with a blessing from God the Father, it may seem mere convention. We need to remember, though, that the Old Testament does not routinely refer to God as Father—not even as Father of Israel. The contrast between the Hebrew Scriptures and the Christian Greek Scriptures at this point throws a spotlight on the significance of Jesus' revelation of the Fatherhood of God. The emphasis on God as our own individual Father stands in its importance alongside that of Jesus as Messiah, Savior, and Lord. Those motifs hang together as integrally intertwined; and we should keep that point in mind in grappling with atonement.

To show the significance of New Testament authors' calling God "Father," consider two other undeniable emphases of Jesus of Nazareth. A key theme in Jesus' preaching concerned the kingdom of God, as we have already seen. Yet, the portion of the New Testament following the Gospels calls God "Father" more than twice as often as it mentions the kingdom.[10] Similarly, Jesus' favorite designation of himself was "Son of Man." Yet, following the ascension of our Lord, the New Testament mentions the Son of Man only three times.[11] Clearly this title for Jesus—our Lord's favorite—did not resonate nearly as strongly in the early church's memory as did

The First-century Church

his calling God "Father." It seems plain that the Fatherhood of God constituted the central point of Jesus' gospel as remembered by the first-century church.

Two decades after Jesus, Paul wrote, "God has sent the Spirit of his Son into our hearts, crying, 'Abba!'" (Gal. 4:6). A few years later he said, "[W]e cry 'Abba'" (Rom. 8:15). Those two statements suggest that decades after Jesus, people of the first-century church habitually prayed to God the same way Jesus did—as their Abba. The very prayers of the earliest believers embodied an implicit understanding of Jesus' message—our own dear *Abba* has come to draw his alienated children to himself. This understanding of atonement as the Father's reconciling his children to himself does not represent merely one viewpoint among others but Jesus' own Good News.

Every writer in the New Testament referred to this same truth by implication—without exception! Consider these examples:

- The Apostle Paul described God as "the Father of mercies and the God of all consolation" (2 Cor. 1:3).
- Paul appealed to "our God and Father" to guide his steps back to Thessalonica (1 Thess. 3:11).
- James said every good gift comes down from "the Father of lights" who "gave us birth by the word of truth" (Jas. 1:17-18).
- Peter blessed "the God and Father of our Lord Jesus Christ" who "has given us a new birth . . . through the resurrection of Jesus Christ" (1 Pet. 1:3).
- John pointed to the amazing "love the Father has given us, that we should be called children of God" (1 John 3:1).

On and on we could go multiplying instances of New Testament authors calling God our Father and referring to us as his children and to one another as brothers and sisters.

One of the more surprising examples comes from the sermon we know as the Book of Hebrews. This book sets forth the salvation Jesus brought through extensive analogies drawn from the Temple—High Priest, the Mercy Seat and other articles of Temple furniture, sacrifices, the Day of Atonement, and the ritual of the scapegoat. Even this book noted for its extended metaphor of temple ritual and sacrifice also uses family metaphors. The book begins with God as Father and Jesus as his Son (1:1-13). The author calls Jesus "the Son of God" throughout this sermon. He says, "Christ is faithful over God's household as a son" (3:6). Toward the end of the sermon the author even calls us God's children and clearly implies that God is our Father (12:5-11).

Varied New Testament Metaphors of Salvation

METAPHORS	REPRESENTATIVES
Abba	Gal. 4:6, Rom. 8:15
Access to royal throne room	Rom. 5:2; Eph. 2:18, 3:12
Adoption	Rom. 8:15, Gal. 4:5, Eph. 1:5
Bring alive	Col. 2:12, 13
Circumcision	Col. 2:11
Conquering general	Col. 1:13, 20; 2:15
Day of Atonement	Heb. 9:25
Death	Col. 2:20; Rom. 6:3, 11; 7:4; Gal. 2:20
Exodus[12]	Luke 9:31
Justification	Rom. 2:13; 3:(20), 24, 26, 28, 30; 4:5; 5:1, 9, 18; 8:30, 33; Gal. 2:(16), 17; 3:8, 11, 24; 5:4; Titus 3:7; Jas. 2:24
Passover	1 Cor. 5:7, 1 Pet. 1:19
Peace	Acts 10:36, Rom. 5:1, Eph. 2:17, Col. 1:20
Manumission, emancipation	Mark 10:45 = Matt. 20:28, 1 Tim. 2:6
Mercy Seat	Rom. 3:25, Heb. 9:5
Purchase in the market	Gal. 4:5 *(exagaradzo)*
Reconciliation	Rom. 5:10, 11; 2 Cor. 5:18, 19, 20; Col. 1:20, 22; Eph. 2:16
Redeem at a price	Eph. 1:7 *(apolutrosin)*
Redemption	Luke 1:68, 2:38, 21:28, 24:21; Rom. 3:24, 8:1; 1 Cor. 1:30; Eph. 1:7, 14; 4:30; Col. 1:14; Titus 2:14; Heb. 9:12, 15; 1 Pet. 1:18
Regeneration, new birth	Titus 3:5, Jas. 1:17-18, 1 Pet. 1:3, 23
Resurrection	Rom. 6:4, Col. 3:1
Sacrifice, blood	Eph. 5:2; Heb. 7:27, 9:11-10:12
Scapegoat	Heb. 13:12
Triumphal procession	2 Cor. 2:14–16, Col. 2:15, Eph. 4:8

Sacrifice

Only one other metaphor found almost universal popularity among first-century believers: sacrifice. First-century Palestinian Jews were obsessed with the Jerusalem Temple and its sacrificial rituals. We should not be surprised, therefore, that sacrificial imagery should loom so large in the way the earliest believers described the significance of Jesus' life and death.

His crucifixion took place during the Passover festival. The Gospel According to John takes pains to make sure we know that Jesus was crucified precisely during the slaughter of the Paschal lambs. With this connection to Passover, it comes as a surprise that the concept of Jesus' death as a Passover sacrifice does not appear in the New Testament more often than it does. John the Baptist proclaimed Jesus as "the Lamb of God who takes away the sin of the world" (John 1:29). Paul wrote to the Corinthians, "For Christ, our Passover lamb, has been sacrificed" (1 Cor. 5:7). The Book of Revelation refers to Jesus as "the Lamb" several times, presumably alluding to the Passover lambs. 1 Peter 1:19 alludes to Christ's death as a Passover sacrifice. Those four examples, surprisingly, exhaust the New Testament use of the Passover metaphor. The metaphors of redemption and reconciliation appear far more often and in just as many authors.

The Book of Hebrews is the only New Testament work to draw out an extended metaphor of Jesus' death in sacrificial language, but it alludes to the Day of Atonement rather than Passover. Other sacrificial allusions are much briefer. In Ephesians we read, "Christ loved us and gave himself up for us, a fragrant offering and sacrifice to God" (5:2). Sacrificial imagery also occurs in Acts 8:32; 2 Cor. 5:21; 1 Peter 1:2, 19; and 1 John 2:2 and 4:10. These illustrative metaphors of sacrifice constitute most of the explicit uses of such language to illustrate the meaning of Christ's death. Oblique statements such as that Jesus "offered" himself or "gave" himself for us or mentioning his saving us by his blood add indirect sacrificial metaphors. References to the blood of Christ, however, may not in every case equal a sacrificial metaphor. These instances may refer to the literal blood of his scourging and cross or as a synecdoche (a part representing the whole) indicating Jesus' death.

Sacrificial metaphors do occur in most New Testament authors—James and Jude being notable exceptions. That almost universal pattern indicates the early church did think of Jesus' death under the metaphor of sacrifice more often than under any other except that of the loving Father's free forgiveness and reception of us into his family. We should expect this pattern in view of the overarching significance of the Temple and its sacrifices for their lives prior to the advent of Jesus of Nazareth. (See "Varied New Testament Metaphors of Salvation," p. 56.)

Then what did the sacrificial metaphor mean? Jews had dealt with sin by offering animal sacrifices in the Temple. References to Christ's death as a sacrifice pointed to the extremely costly nature of the Father's forgiveness. Divine mercy does not come cheap. It cost God in Christ everything (2 Cor. 5:14).

Still, even when using the metaphor of sacrifice, the New Testament never speaks of the cross as propitiating God or even reconciling God to us. When Jesus preached what God was doing in himself, implying his messiahship and deity, he faced certain death in Roman-occupied Judea. Facing the cross, he went forward with redemptive love and grace. His sacrificial death did not secure God's forgiveness; but rather, it revealed God's grace and pursuit of humanity without limits. Then his resurrection revealed and bestowed God's forgiveness on humanity, who murdered God's ultimate self-revelation.

Redemption

The third most widely used metaphor for what we have received in Jesus is that of redemption. This study has argued throughout that Jesus' metaphor of God as our *Abba* drew its communicative and emotive power for first-century Jews from two intricately connected Hebraic cultural concepts: (1) the idea that God as Israel's "Father" redeemed (emancipated) them from slavery in the Exodus and in their return from Exile and (2) the picture of God as their near-kin Redeemer in both historical acts. The evidence from the New Testament for the thinking and teaching of the earliest disciples of Jesus indicates they saw clearly the implications of his teaching.

The words for redeem and redemption appear rarely in the Gospels—actually, only four times in Luke[13] in addition to Mark 10:45 and Matthew 20:28. Still, the words for redemption rank as the third most widely used first-century Christian metaphor of atonement.[14] The twenty occurrences of this word-group account for more instances and more authors than any New Testament metaphor other than Father and sacrifice. (See "Key New Testament Metaphors of Salvation," p. 60.) This word and concept evidently resonated widely in the first-century church. This resonance no doubt came from first century believers' recognition that Jesus' metaphor of God as Father recalled connections to ideas from the heart of their national history and culture.

So, what does redemption mean in the New Testament? Most biblical commentators say the word means ransom or simply liberation. I am convinced a richer, more historically allusive meaning attaches to that word. Luke used redemption vocabulary four times in his gospel to translate Aramaic quotations of Jesus and those associated with him. Since Luke also included an explicit reference to the Exodus in his transfiguration narrative, it seems he understood his redemption vocabulary as an implied analogy to God's liberation of Israel in the Exodus. That is how the Old Testament authors frequently used the word.[15]

Those same Old Testament passages, furthermore, repeatedly cited the Exodus as God's near-kin redemption of his people—God was Israel's Redeemer. I, therefore, take Luke's usage of redemption vocabulary to imply not only a parallel with the Exodus but also to imply that God is our near-kin Redeemer. Luke made that implication clear when Zechariah, employing a family metaphor, said God "has come and has redeemed his people" (Luke 1:78).

In addition, Mark's use of the word often translated "ransom" (Mark 10:45 = Matt. 20:28) probably has that same connotation. Mark's Greek word *lutron* carried in the first century the meaning price of manumission, or emancipation, of a slave (not our concept of ransom), which would have immediately called to mind for Jews Israel's liberation from slavery in the Exodus.

Most examples of redemption language in the New Testament appear to reflect at least the frequent use of that vocabulary in the Greek version of the Old Testament to refer to Israel's redemption by Yahweh, the Redeemer, both in the Exodus and in the return from exile. Furthermore, at least six times these words refer explicitly and unmistakably to near-kin redemption in saying that God the Father has redeemed for himself a people or a possession.[16] These occurrences would call to any Jewish mind the use of this same word group in Deuteronomy, Isaiah, and Jeremiah to refer to Israel's redemption from slavery in the Exodus and from exile in their return. This implication of Jesus' calling God "Father" struck the earliest Christians so forcefully, they remembered it and even used the distinctive vocabulary for that concept in communicating the gospel.

We should also note that the New Testament never calls either Jesus or God our Redeemer. That absence of usage contrasts strikingly with the Old Testament's frequent reference to God as Israel's Redeemer. Authors call Jesus our "redemption" in a couple of places (1 Cor. 1:30, Heb. 9:15), but never "Redeemer." Apparently well aware that Yahweh was Israel's Redeemer, they did not transfer that title to Jesus, instead calling Jesus our "redemption"—the deliverance sent by the Father. (Readers desiring more specific discussion of the New Testament's use of redemption language should see the appendices "Old Testament Redemption Vocabulary," p. 116, and "New Testament Redemption Vocabulary," p. 120.)

Key New Testament Metaphors of Salvation

WORKS	FATHER	REDEEM	RECONCILE

Luke-Acts	Acts 1:4, 7; 2:33	*lutroo* (vb.)[17]
		  Luke 1:68, 2:38,
		  24:21 24
		
		apolutrosis (n.)
		  Luke 21:28
		
		exodon (n.)
		  Luke 9:31	

Pauline Epistles	*Pater*:
	  3 times in Rom.
	  3 times in 1 Cor.
	  5 times in 2 Cor.
	  3 times in Gal.
	  3 times in Phil.
	  4 times in 1 Thess.
	  1 time in Philem.
	  8 times in Eph.
	  4 times in Col.
	  3 times in 2 Thess.
	  1 time in 1 Tim.
	  1 time in 2 Tim.
	  1 time in Titus
	
	Abba:
	  Gal. 4:6, Rom. 8:15
		apolutrosis (n.)
		  Rom. 3:24, 8:23;
		  1 Cor. 1:30; Eph. 1:7,
		  14, 4:30; Col. 1:14
		
		exagarazo (vb.)
		  Gal. 3:13, 4:5
		
		lutroo (vb.)
		  Titus 2:14
			katallasso (vb.)
			  Rom. 5:10, 11;
			  2 Cor. 5:18, 19,
			  20; Eph. 2:16;
			  Col. 1:20, 21
			
			katallage (n.)
			  Rom. 5:11,
			  11:15; 2 Cor.
			  5:18, 19

Hebrews	1:5, 2:6, 12:9	*lutrosis* (n.)
		  9:12
		
		apolutrosis (n.)
		  9:15, 11:35	

James	1:17, 27; 3:9		
Petrine Epistles	1 Pet. 1:2, 3, 17; 2 Pet. 1:17	*lutroo* (vb.) 1 Pet. 1:18	
Johannine Epistles	12 times in 1 John 4 times in 2 John		
Jude	1		
Revelation	1:6; 2:27; 3:5, 21; 14:1		

Clear Multiple Echoes of Jesus' Teaching

In addition to the individual metaphors of Father and redemption, several times New Testament authors merge the metaphors of Father, new birth or adoption, family, and redemption in such a way as to show this combination of ideas circulated widely in the early church. A clear reflection of the language and thought of Jesus at multiple levels occurs in 1 Peter. In the first chapter, Peter said his readers call on God as Father (vv. 2, 17) and then moved immediately to say they had been "redeemed" (v. 18). Then he proceeded quickly to say they had been "born anew" (v. 23). Thus, Peter joins the concepts of God as Father, new birth into God's family, and redemption.

Furthermore, it is probably not coincidental that he refers directly to their "exile" (v. 17). His description of Christ as a "lamb without defect or blemish" refers to Christ as their Passover Lamb, an oblique reference to the Exodus. When we remember that the Old Testament repeatedly described Israel's exodus from Egypt and their return from exile as their redemption and God as their near-kin Redeemer, the joining of these themes becomes all the more striking.

For a second example, Paul said in Galatians 4:4-7 that Jesus came "to redeem those who were under the law" so that we might be adopted as God's children. For this reason, we cry out "*Abba*! Father!" Paul's word translated "redeem" here means a marketplace purchase, approximately the meaning of one of the two Hebrew words (*padah*, purchase) used to describe God's redemption of Israel from Egypt and Babylon. Because of the strong emphasis on God as Father and us as his children, near-kin redemption is probably intended here as well, even though he did not use the distinctive Greek word for that concept here. A few years later, though, in writing to the Romans, he combined the same complex of ideas in Roman 8:14-23—God as our *Abba* (v. 15), us as God's adopted children (vv. 14, 15, 16, 17, 19, 21), and our redemption (v. 23). In this passage he did use the distinctive Greek word that indicated near-kin redemption in the LXX.

For a fourth example, Ephesians 1:1-14 speaks of God as "our Father" (v. 2) and of us as God's adopted children (1:5) who have "redemption through his blood" (v. 7) and "redemption as God's own people" (v. 14). In this passage the author combines the sacrificial metaphor with the familial metaphor of God our Father who has given Jesus as our redemption. Here, the word translated "redemption" is the Greek word that frequently means in the Septuagint near-kin redemption. When used in close connection with God as our Father and us as God's children, this word obviously carries that implication. We find a fifth example in Colossians 1:12-22. This passage merges God as Father, with Exodus allusions, redemption, and reconciliation.

For a sixth example, the epistle of Titus opens with a benediction from "God the Father" (1:4) and then states that God's grace "has appeared bringing salvation to all" (2:11). The author then spells out how God's grace has become effective for us: Jesus "gave himself for us that he might redeem us . . . and purify for himself a people of his own" (2:14). Here we have the combination of God as Father and redemption of God's people. Surely God's near-kin redemption of his people through Jesus shines clearly here. In Titus as in Ephesians and 1 Peter, we can easily miss the significance of calling God "Father" in the blessing. We tend to treat that designation as routine, forgetting it was anything but conventional in the first-century Jewish context.

Thus, either two or possibly five different New Testament authors (according to our attribution of the authorship of Ephesians, Colossians, and Titus[18]) combine God as Father with redemption. This combination supports our contention that the first-century church understood Jesus' metaphor of God as Father to imply near-kin redemption, parallel to Old Testament references to God's redeeming Israel from Egypt and from exile.

Two other metaphors of our salvation through Jesus Christ are notable enough that we should give special attention to them, both unique to the Apostle Paul.

Justification

We are all so aware of Paul's courtroom metaphor of justification that many people seem to think that word constitutes Paul's sole concept of atonement. Actually, Paul rarely used either the word "justify" or the concept outside of Galatians and Romans, elsewhere generating a host of other metaphors to illustrate what Jesus did for us. Furthermore, no one else in the New Testament employed the metaphor of justification to illustrate our salvation through Jesus Christ. James used the word but only to rebut a misunderstanding of Paul.

Second only to his emphasis on the Father, Paul seized on a concept from the Old Testament to teach his understanding of the salvation Christ brought. The concept of justification occurs repeatedly in several different senses in the Hebrew Scriptures and also in the Greek Septuagint and the Apocrypha (highly regarded religious works not accepted by the Jews as Scripture). In the first century, justification served as a courtroom term approximately equivalent to our legal word "acquit." Justification, though, meant more than to declare "not guilty." It meant to declare "righteous"—"in the right." Paul commandeered this word to present a powerful metaphor of atonement: God declares us right with himself. But how?

In Romans, Paul answers the implied questions, "Who are the people of God? Who does God declare righteous, right with himself?"[19] Paul glides over the "barbarians" with a bare mention (1:14). Then he dismisses people of wisdom (philosophy) in relatively short order (1:18-31). Then he declares that people of Torah (Law), the Jews, are not the people of God, no matter what his own people may claim (2:1-3:20). He then arrives at his climax—people of faith constitute the true people of God (3:21-4:25). God declares all people of faith righteous—right with himself.

Although Protestants have elevated Paul's forensic metaphor to the status of the most important of doctrines, justification seems to have been a picture unique to Paul. No one else used it to explain what Jesus brought us. We tend to think Paul thought of salvation only in terms of justification, but that idea could not be farther from the truth. In Romans alone, for instance, Paul used at least twelve different metaphors to illustrate what God did for us in Jesus Christ. While justification did hold a privileged position in Paul's lexicon of metaphors, it does not rank as one of the major metaphors in the wider New Testament. It appears we have given the apostle's metaphor more significance that even Paul gave it, certainly than the New Testament gave it.

Moreover, we should not take Paul's metaphor of justification to mean that in the death of Christ a price has been paid that makes it possible for God to forgive us. The full importance of Paul's concept of justification shines through in Romans 5 when he moves almost imperceptibly from the metaphor of justification to that of peace. "Therefore, since we are justified by faith, we have peace with God through our Lord Jesus Christ," Paul wrote (v. 1). Peace with God is the point of justification. He went on to write, "God proves his love for us in that while we still were sinners Christ died for us" (v. 8). Christ's death did not make God's love for us possible; the cross flowed from God's prior love that sent Christ into the world as his highest self-revelation. Then Paul morphed from his discussion of justification into the concept of reconciliation.

Reconciliation

"For if while we were enemies, we were reconciled to God through the death of his Son," Paul wrote following his extensive discussion of justification, "much more surely, having been reconciled, will we be saved by his life. But more than that, we even boast in God through our Lord Jesus Christ, through whom we have now received reconciliation" (5:10-11). God was not reconciled to us through the cross of Christ; we were reconciled to God. God did not change; we did.

Surprisingly, considering the confusion the word atonement has occasioned in the church, that English word appears only once in the King James Version of the New Testament.[20] Everywhere else, the translators rendered that same Greek word as "reconciliation." Of course, atonement—at-one-ment—actually means reconciliation.[21] If we want to be true to the New Testament, we should speak of atonement as reconciliation—of us to God by faith. Significantly, the only other way Paul used the word reconcile dealt with a family situation—a wife reconciling to her husband.[22] With the word reconciliation, we are back in a relational context of thought rather than a legal or ritualistic one. Even when using the courtroom metaphor, Paul reaches the climax of his thought with a relational metaphor. Atonement—reconciliation—is relational, not legal, forensic, or economic (having to do with a debt).

Like justification, reconciliation (atonement) seems to have been a word unique to Paul.[23] Notice, though, that Paul asserted that God reconciles us to himself. In 2 Corinthians 5:20 he even challenged believers to "be reconciled to God." He never said that God reconciled himself to us. The change in reconciliation—in atonement—takes place in us, not in God. God does not need to change; we do. (See "Key New Testament Metaphors of Salvation," p. 60.) Note that Paul finds no tension within God that makes it difficult for him to forgive.

In the first chapter of Colossians, for a third example, discussion of Christ's "redemption" by "the Father" moves to its grand climax in reconciliation with God through the cross (1:12-22). Three different epistles of the Pauline literature portray what we have received in Christ as reconciliation with God. Furthermore, the last example ties reconciliation to the Father's redemption.

Significantly, Paul reversed the prior usage of this word among Jews. In 2 Maccabees, the Greek words for reconcile and reconciliation refer to God's forsaking his anger and reconciling himself to his people.[24] In other words, God was propitiated, appeased, and therefore changed his attitude. The ancient rabbis and Josephus regularly used those words to mean "appease."[25]

Paul reversed that idea, saying that God "reconciled us to himself" and calls us to "be reconciled to God" (2 Cor. 5:18, 19, 21). Paul in 2 Corinthians 5 and Romans 5, like Colossians 1, possibly deliberately contradicted 2 Maccabees and insisted God does not need to reconcile himself to us, but we need to reconcile to God. Atonement means our reconciliation to God, not some event that changes God's mind about us. God was never against us. Paul even wrote that "we were enemies" of God (2 Cor. 5:10) who were reconciled to God; God was never our enemy who needed propitiation. God declares us right with himself when we reconcile to him in faith and faithfulness.

We should note, further, that in Romans Paul combines the concepts of justification, adoption, God as our *Abba*, reconciliation, redemption, and deliverance almost interchangeably in a single chapter. Romans 8 opens with the statement that we have been "set free" in Christ Jesus (v. 2), then moves on to say we have been adopted as children and cry *Abba* (v. 15) as the family of God ("children" vv. 16, 21; "heirs" v. 17), and are awaiting our ultimate "adoption," namely "the redemption of the body" (v. 23). He then makes another allusion to our being in God's family ("brothers" v. 29) and concludes the passage with the theme of "justification" (v. 30). Even when developing his metaphor of justification, Paul reverted to his favorite metaphor of familial relationship, calling God "Father." Atonement is a relationship, not a transaction or a deal or a payoff.

Paul's words reconcile and reconciliation in connection with *Abba* (Father) possibly grasp the heart of Jesus' gospel more than any other concept in the New Testament. The parable of the prodigal son describes reconciliation. Jesus' central message called us to reconcile with the Father. When we remember that the word "atonement" actually means reconciliation, it becomes apparent that we have spun our wheels needlessly for centuries with all our theories of the atonement. Atonement is simply about reconciling with the Father—nothing more, nothing less, nothing else.

Multiple Metaphors, but Not Theories

The first-century church created many picturesque illustrations of the salvation we have in Christ in addition to the five most popular ones described here, but none of those twenty-plus imaginative allusions amounted to explanations of atonement. Nowhere does the New Testament ever attempt to provide some literal, legal theory of how the cross made it possible for a wrathful God to change from our enemy to our Father and to forgive our sin. Their metaphors illustrated the saving work of Jesus, making it come alive in the imaginations of early believers out of their cultural experience.

Admittedly, not every metaphor of salvation created by the early church can be subsumed under that of God as Father. Those other metaphors derived from a variety of sources such as temple and sacrifices, courtroom, marketplace, battlefield, military parades, Exodus, return from exile, birth, family life, and death. Furthermore, their metaphors were not always consistent with one another. The Fatherhood of God does represent, however, the dominant metaphor in the early church following the example of the Lord—so dominant that it became universal. For that reason, for the last 1,800 years we have missed it as Jesus' own metaphor for the Good News he proclaimed.

Its universality shines forth in that every New Testament author used it. Its dominant position in the lexicon of early church metaphors displays itself in that whatever other metaphor an author may have been developing at the moment, he tended to lapse back into that family metaphor. He would refer to God as "Father," to us as God's "children," or to fellow believers as "brothers." If these uses seem too ordinary to be significant, then we must remind ourselves that those metaphors were not ordinary among Jews prior to Jesus. Even the author of Hebrews setting forth the cross in terms of the Day of Atonement lapsed into such family language several times. Even Paul setting forth the cross in courtroom language progressed to speak of peace and reconciliation—terms signally suitable for family usage. "Father" may not have been the only metaphor the earliest Christians used; but it was their most common, most universal, and best loved one.

Then What Went Wrong?

If Jesus and the earliest believers preached such a simple and beautiful gospel, how did it happen that for the past several centuries believers have hardly known what to do with the doctrine of atonement? The answer to that question is an 1,800-year-long story that began in the late second century after Christ. The next three chapters will narrate the story of how the church forgot our Lord's central message that God is our loving Father who calls us to return to fellowship with him. With that loss, it found itself under the necessity of creating various theories of the atonement.

Notes

[1] Word counts cannot substitute for detailed analysis of ideas in the biblical text; they can, however, serve as a useful proxy for the relative importance of certain ideas. A full discussion of this vocabulary appears in *Theological Dictionary of the New Testament*, ed. Gerhard Kittel (Grand Rapids: Eerdmans, 1965), 3:300-323. This article along with my own research provides much of the material in this chapter.

[2] Those four favorite words for propitiation were ’εξιλασκομαι (*exilaskomai*), ’εξιλασμος (*exilasmos*), ’εξιλασις (*exilasis*), and ’εξιλασμα (*exilasma*). These four words appear in the Septuagint 122 times by my count, translating a number of different Hebrew words. We find them an additional 18 times in the Apocrypha. (See "Propitiation in the Septuagint and New Testament" in Chapter 6.)

[3] The first of those two minor Greek words, ‘ιλασμος (*hilasmos*), we find with five different meanings: atonement, restitution or propitiation, forgiveness, and sin offering. The second of those two words, ‘ιλασκομαι (*hilaskomai*), appears with three different meanings. It translates Hebrew words meaning forgive, cover or atone, and repent. Only in Num. 5:8, possibly, and in a Greek section of the Apocrypha following Est. 4:17 that is not in the Hebrew does it mean "propitiation" or "be propitious." (See "Propitiation in the Septuagint and New Testament" in Chapter 6.)

[4] We find ‘ιλασμος (*hilasmos*) in 1 John 2:2 and 4:10, where it clearly means, from comparison with its usage in the Septuagint, the general concept of "sin offering" or "sacrifice of atonement"—not the highly specific "propitiation" as in the King James Version. The second word, ‘ιλασκομαι (*hilaskomai*), appears in Luke 18:13 where in Jesus' parable the publican prays, "God, be *merciful* to me, a sinner!" In that usage it is parallel to several verses in the LXX. We find it a second time in Hebrews 2:17 where the author says Jesus made "a sacrifice of atonement" or "a sin offering for the sins of the people." That is, from comparison with the LXX we cannot give it more than a very general sense rather than the highly specific meaning of "propitiation."

[5] That word, ‘ιλαστηριον (*hilasterion*), appears only in Rom. 3:25 and Heb. 9:5. It occurs at least twenty-seven times in the Septuagint and always means either the Mercy Seat, the ledge around

the altar, or some article or architectural feature of the Temple—*never* "propitiation." It, therefore, obviously means Mercy Seat in both Romans and Hebrews—that is, the place where sin is removed. (See "Propitiation in the Septuagint and New Testament" in Chapter 6.)

[6]The Hebrew word *kaphar* and its derivatives in its sacrificial usage were translated by 'εξιλασκομαι/*exilaskomai* 83 out of 100 times in the Septuagint, *never* by 'ιλασκομαι/*hilaskomai*.

[7]The Greek term *hilasterion* never appears in the Septuagint in the sense of propitiation, but always without exception in the sense of Mercy Seat (overwhelmingly), or the ledge of the altar (three times), or the capital of a pillar (once).

[8]Other than Jesus' comments in the Gospels, the New Testament refers to God as "Father" more than 70 times. This frequent usage compares strikingly to 24 references to the cross or to "crucified" and 33 mentions of sacrifice or blood, outside the Gospels' passion narratives.

[9]No less than 41 times.

[10]The Kingdom mentioned 29 times compared with God as Father more than 70 times.

[11]Only in Acts 7:56; Rev. 1:13, 14:14.

[12]This reference represents metaphors of salvation by the evangelist Luke, not Jesus, although in a gospel.

[13]Luke 1:68, 2:38, 21:28, 24:21 use the λυτροω (*lutroo*) word-group.

[14]The *lutroo* word-group.

[15]I refer here to the Greek Septuagint's usage of the λυτροω (*lutroo*) word-group to translate the two Hebrew words *padah* (ransom, redeem) and *ga'al* (near-kin redemption).

[16]Luke 1:68; Rom. 8:12-23; Eph. 1:2, 7-14; Col. 1:2, 12-23; Titus 2:14; and 1 Pet. 1:2, 17-19.

[17]These references represent metaphors of salvation by people other than Jesus himself (with one exception, Luke 21:28), even though from the Gospels.

[18]A majority of critical scholars attribute Ephesians, Colossians, and Titus to disciples of Paul rather than to the Apostle himself.

[19]For this idea I am indebted to N.T. Wright's marvelous commentary on Romans in *The New Interpreter's Bible*, vol. 10 (Nashville: Abingdon, 2002), where he at least implies this understanding of Romans.

[20]Rom. 5:11, where the NRSV says "reconciliation," as above. The NIV uses it twice (Heb. 2:17, 9:5). The RSV, the NRSV, and the ASV never use that contentious word in the New Testament.

[21]The Greek words are καταλλαγη / καταλασσω (*katallage* / *katallasso*) and 'αποκαταλλαγη / 'αποκαταλλασσω (*apokatalage* / *apokatallasso*), both built on the word 'αλλασσω (*allasso*), meaning "to change." The addition of the prepositions to the beginning of the root word make it mean "reconcile, reconciliation."

[22]See 1 Cor. 7:11.

[23]Paul's nine uses of this verb (καταλασσω) and its related noun concerning atonement are as follows: Rom. 5:10 (twice), 11; 11:15; 2 Cor. 5:18 (twice), 19 (twice), 20. The similar word 'αποκαταλασσω appears in Col. 1:20, 22 and Eph. 2:16, bringing the total uses of the words reconcile and reconciliation in the New Testament to 12, in five passages in the Pauline literature.

[24]See 2 Macc. 1:5, 5:20, 7:33, 8:29. These are the only places this word occurs in the Septuagint.

[25]See Friedrich Buchsel, *Theological Dictionary of the New Testament*, ed. Gerhard Kittel (Grand Rapids: Eerdmans, 1965), 1:254-259.

Chapter 7

Migration Away from Jesus' Good News

From the second century onward, the Gentile Greek-speaking church lost a full understanding of the implications of Jesus' calling God "Abba" and therefore produced interpretations of atonement radically at odds with the revelation taught by Jesus.

The Great Amnesia

The first-century church as reflected in the New Testament did not write about "the atonement." We only find an equivalent for the word atonement in the Apostle Paul's letters (and possibly in those of his disciples). Even in the Pauline literature, the word we could translate atonement means reconciliation rather than our technical theological word for a doctrine. Furthermore, the early church did not limit Christ's saving work to his death on the cross. Nor did the church teach that the cross somehow made it possible for God to forgive our sin. They did, of course, see Jesus' great redemptive work as climaxed and sealed in his death and resurrection. After all, each of the four gospels devotes approximately a third of its space to the passion week. Some interpreters have even described the gospels as "passion narratives with extended introductions."

Still, Jesus' death and resurrection were seen as a part of—the climax of—his entire life viewed as a whole. Because of their immersion in Jewish culture, the first generations of believers intuitively grasped Jesus' message that God was their loving *Abba* who had sent his Son to liberate his beloved children. They did not need to offer any particular "theory" of the atonement, and they did not. They simply proclaimed that their heavenly Father was reconciling his alienated children to himself through his embodiment in his Son.

Then disaster struck the adolescent church in the crushing military might of the Roman armies. In 70 CE, Titus besieged Jerusalem, breached its three walls, and destroyed the city and its temple. The Jewish church in Jerusalem survived until the rebellion of Bar Kochba in 132 CE. By this time, the Romans had had their fill of the rebellious, ungovernable Jews. Emperor Hadrian's army totally razed Jerusalem and renamed it *Aelia Capitolina*. In that name he combined one of his own names with the joint title of three Roman deities—Jupiter, Juno, and Minerva—the perfect insult to Jews.

From that date, Jewish Jerusalem ceased to exist, as did the Jewish church in Jerusalem.[1] After 135 CE the leadership of the Palestinian church became Gentile. Greek-speaking and philosophically educated Gentiles moved into the leadership of the Christian church all over the world. Pockets of Jewish Christianity survived, but predominantly Jewish leadership of the church ceased.

Many of the new Gentile converts to the faith had been educated in Greek philosophy. The intellectual authorities for this new leadership consisted of Plato, Epicurus, Zeno, and Pythagoras from the deep past. By the third century, their more recent authorities had become Plotinus and Porphyry, the inventor and the popularizer of Neo-Platonism. They spoke Greek and thought as cultural Greeks. When they read the Hebrew and Christian Scriptures, they read them through the lens of Plato, Aristotle, Zeno, and Porphyry.

In the second century, the church exhibited contradictory views of the philosophers. Some accepted various strands of Greek philosophy, while other rejected the philosophers as pagan and false, and still others accepted them as preparatory to Christianity.[2] Tertullian, for instance, could ostensibly reject Greek philosophy by asking, "What has Athens to do with Jerusalem?"[3] At the same time, while rejecting Plato's doctrine of the soul, he nevertheless thought of the soul in terms taught him by other philosophers and debated its nature in those terms. Even the early fathers of the church who thought they rejected the philosophers as foreign to their faith just as often had no idea how many ideas of the philosophers they had brought with them into their new faith.

While not overtly teaching the doctrines of the philosophers, they intuitively incorporated into their theology the philosophical ideas and definitions in which they had been reared. That unconscious practice changed the nature of their message profoundly. At the beginning of the third century, for instance, Origen adopted a generally Platonic conception of the cosmos and of the soul.[4] By the time of Augustine of Hippo at the turn of the fourth and fifth centuries, Christian theology had become largely neo-Platonic. This neo-Platonic influence remained in the church in the following centuries and still comes down to us in many ways in our own day.

Many of the church leaders would eventually speak Latin and think as cultural Romans in terms of the Roman nobility (the hierarchy—the "princes of the church"), the emperor (the pope—the "Pontifex Maximus," a title borrowed from the Caesars), and the empire (the hierarchy itself). In time, the Latin church produced the Roman Catholic Church.

Without realizing their error, the church leaders innocently interpreted the teachings of the Hebrew prophets, Jesus of Nazareth, and the Christian Greek Scriptures as if Plato had been among the prophets and Plotinus and Porphyry two of the Apostles. Much of the Hebraic meaning of the gospel fell by the wayside. They interpreted the New Testament using the definitions of Greek words inherited from the philosophers. By the time of Augustine's death, the church had entered its "Great Amnesia," from which we are still in the early stages of awakening.[5]

Early Second-century Preaching

Through much of the second century we do not witness in the surviving record any concerted effort to explain the atonement. The writings of the church fathers we possess simply assert that we receive salvation through Jesus and his sufferings and blood.[6] By the second century, church leaders had lost for the most part any major emphasis on God as our own personal Father. They did continue to speak of God as Father, but by this term they meant either our Creator, or the Father of Jesus Christ, or the Father in various trinitarian formulae.[7] Only rarely do we encounter such expressions as "we from Christ ... are called and are the true sons of God."[8] Irenaeus spoke of our "adoption of sons" and receiving the "gift of adoption."[9] Clement of Alexandria even said "we, too, are first born sons."[10] Such statements as these, however, are notable for their exceeding rarity.

The incarnation of God in Christ sometimes took center stage in their teaching on atonement. For example, Ignatius said we are "saved through union with Jesus Christ."[11] Irenaeus wrote that we are redeemed "by means of communion with God."[12] They did not settle on a single explanatory theory as to how Jesus saves us. They could speak of Jesus as "liberating us,"[13] or "reconciling us to God,"[14] or "propitiating"[15] God for us. They used various metaphors from time to time, but mostly they simply said we are saved by Jesus Christ. Some of them, however, decided they needed a more precise understanding of how Jesus' life, teachings, death, and resurrection provided salvation.

The Great Confusion

We see the early beginning of a new way of thinking in the anonymous Epistle to Diognetus (ca. 130) that said God "gave His own Son as a ransom for us,"[16] without indicating that the ransom was paid to anyone. This statement possibly harked back to Mark 10:45 / Matthew 20:28 (echoed by 1 Tim. 2:6). A few years later, Irenaeus (130–202) said repeatedly that "the Word" has "redeemed" us.[17] From the tenor of his comments and since his Latin word for redeemed meant ransomed, we can conclude Irenaeus was beginning to construct a theory of the atonement from Mark's word frequently translated "ransom" (Mark 10:45). He did not see the word "ransom" as metaphorical but as literal, legal, and transactional.

The "Great Confusion" had begun. Tertullian (155–240) followed suit and further debased Irenaeus' conception of the ransom. Also writing in Latin, Tertullian continued

Irenaeus' theme of Christ's "ransoming" us. He created the idea that in Adam's fall Satan robbed God of "His own image and likeness," which God had to recover through the ransom of Christ. Because of Christ's ransom, "hell re-transferred the right it had in us, and our covenant is in heaven."[18] Origen (ca. 184–253) then carried the ransom to the devil idea to its ultimate extreme, describing God as outwitting Satan into accepting a ransom God would then slyly take back in the Resurrection. God engaged in a duplicitous fraud and cheated the Devil out of the souls of men![19]

Thus, the concept of the atonement as a ransom paid to the devil entered the church and became one of the favored ways of explaining the atonement for centuries. Later theologians enlarged on Origen's theory to a disturbing extent. Some subsequent theologians who kept the ransom concept balked at the idea of the ransom being paid to Satan. While the church could never settle on the question of to whom the ransom was paid, the general idea of the ransom theory stayed alive in the church for centuries and remained the most common explanation until Anselm in 1097. (See Chapter 8.)

Rise of the Ransom Theory

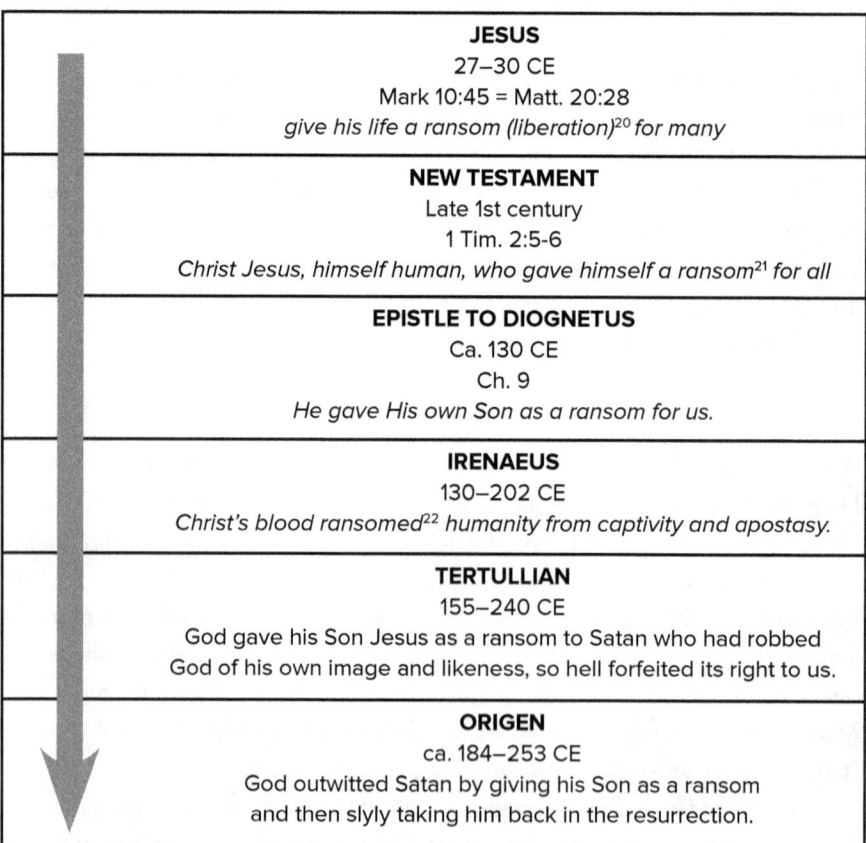

JESUS
27–30 CE
Mark 10:45 = Matt. 20:28
give his life a ransom (liberation)[20] for many

NEW TESTAMENT
Late 1st century
1 Tim. 2:5-6
Christ Jesus, himself human, who gave himself a ransom[21] for all

EPISTLE TO DIOGNETUS
Ca. 130 CE
Ch. 9
He gave His own Son as a ransom for us.

IRENAEUS
130–202 CE
Christ's blood ransomed[22] humanity from captivity and apostasy.

TERTULLIAN
155–240 CE
God gave his Son Jesus as a ransom to Satan who had robbed God of his own image and likeness, so hell forfeited its right to us.

ORIGEN
ca. 184–253 CE
God outwitted Satan by giving his Son as a ransom and then slyly taking him back in the resurrection.

Other Views of the Fathers

Athanasius (296–373), for one example, did not buy into the ransom theory. He saw the atonement as effected in the incarnation itself. Borrowing from Plato's ideas, he envisioned the Word in becoming Jesus of Nazareth as taking on our human nature (which he saw as actually existing apart from any individual human beings) and thereby lifting human nature up to God, deifying human nature itself.[23] Plato, Plotinus, and Porphyry had now become inspired apostles!

Whatever explanation any given theologian gave of the salvation Christ proclaimed, the church had lost contact with its Hebraic roots. Ambrose (340–397) could say concerning Luke 2:38 that Anna announced that "the Redeemer of all people has come."[24] That eminent preacher did not notice that the New Testament never calls Jesus "Redeemer," that Scripture only calls Yahweh "Redeemer." Because of their ignorance of the cultural background of redemption language, the church fathers created all sorts of alien explanations of our salvation. Augustine of Hippo (354–430) represented the best in late fourth-century interpretation in understanding redemption to mean rescue and deliverance.[25] Few of the church fathers, however, displayed as much biblical erudition as Augustine, although this eminent theologian all too often developed his doctrines in neo-Platonic terms.

From the second century onward, the Greek church variously simplified redemption into salvation, or explained it in philosophical terms borrowed from Plato as Jesus deifying human nature, or corrupted it into a ransom to Satan, or dropped both the word and the idea altogether. Ever since the Great Amnesia began, Christian theologians have struggled to recover a widely acceptable understanding of exactly how Jesus reconciled humanity to the Father.

A couple of centuries after Augustine of Hippo, a Frankish king began a process that would in time produce the cultural context for the most popular statement of the gospel among many churches today. We turn now to that story—the back story of the understanding of the atonement held by multitudes of Christians of our own day.

Notes

[1] For this story see Hershel Shanks, ed., *Christianity and Rabbinic Judaism* (Biblical Archaeology Society, 1992), 124-149, and also Shanks, *Partings: How Judaism and Christianity Became Two* (Washington, DC: Biblical Archaeology Society, 2013); Diarmaid MacCulloch, *Christianity: The First Three Thousand Years* (New York: Viking, 2009), 106-111.

[2] MacCulloch, *The First Three Thousand Years*, 141-147.

[3] Tertullian, "The Prescription Against Heretics," vol. 7, *The Ante-Nicene Fathers*, ed. Alexander Roberts and James Donalson (Grand Rapids: Eerdmans, 1968), 3:246.

[4] Williston Walker, *A History of the Christian Church* (New York: Charles Scribner's Sons, 1959), 74-76.

Abba, *Father*

⁵Hans Kung, *Christianity: Essence, History, and Future* (New York: Continuum, 1999), 97, 133-134, 169.

⁶ *The Ante-Nicene Fathers*, trans. Alexander Roberts and James Donaldson, ed. A. Cleveland Coxe (Grand Rapids: Eerdmans, 1969), vol. 1. I. Justin Martyr (110–165 C.E.), *Dialogue with Trypho*, 13:200; Irenaeus (120–202 C.E.), *Against Heresies*, 1:527.

⁷Ignatius (30–107), *Epistle to the Ephesians*, ix, Ibid., 53.

⁸Justin Martyr, *Dialogue with Trypho*, cxxxiii, Ibid., 261.

⁹Irenaeus, *Against Heresies*, III.xviii.7, ix.1, Ibid., 448.

¹⁰Clement of Alexandria (153–217), *Exhortation to the Heathen*, ix, Ibid., II, 195.

¹¹Ignatius, *Epistle to the Philadelphians*, v, Ibid., 82.

¹²Irenaeus, Ibid., I.i.1., Ibid., 527.

¹³Irenaeus, Ibid., III.xxiii.2, Ibid., I, 456.

¹⁴Irenaeus, Ibid., V.xiv.2, Ibid., 541.

¹⁵Irenaeus, Ibid., V.xvii.1, Ibid., 544.

¹⁶ *The Ante-Nicene Fathers*, I, 28.

¹⁷Book V.I.1, Ibid., I, 527. We have Irenaeus only in Latin translation for this book, so we do not know what he wrote in his original Greek. His Latin word, however, for "redeemed" (*redemptionem*) actually meant "ransom" or "buying back," not redemption in the Hebraic familial sense.

¹⁸Tertullian, *On the Flesh of Christ*, XVII, *The Ante-Nicene Fathers*, III, 536; *De Fuga in Persecutione*, 12, *The Ante-Nicene Fathers*, IV, 123.

¹⁹Hastings Rashdall, Ibid., 259 fn 2.

²⁰Greek: λυτρον, *lutron*.

²¹Greek: 'αντιλυτρον, *antilutron*.

²²Latin: *redemptionem*.

²³Athanasius, *On the Incarnation* (Louisville, KY: GLH Publishing, 1951), 27.

²⁴ACC-NT, III, 52.

²⁵ACC-NT, IX, 8-9.

Chapter 8

Anselm's Satisfaction Theory

*Anselm explained the gospel in terms borrowed from feudalism:
We have offended God's honor by our sin; his justice demands satisfaction
(compensation) for our offense before he can forgive us.*

Clovis' Problem and *Weregild*

At the astoundingly youthful age of fifteen, the young warrior Clovis succeeded his father as king of the Franks in 481 CE.[1] The boy appears to have been reared in the Germanic religions worshipping Woden, Thor, and Freya (from whom we get the names Wednesday, Thursday, and Friday). He would later marry Clotilde, a Burgundian princess and a Catholic Christian, although her family was Arian. Her family believed Jesus was not eternally the Son of God but became the Son of God by being born God's Son at some point in time. As a Catholic Christian, however, she accepted the Trinitarian doctrine that Father, Son, and Holy Spirit are all three equally and eternally God.

Clotilde tried for years to convert her husband from his pagan upbringing to faith in Jesus Christ, but he resisted. Eventually, in the middle of a battle against his rival Alemanni tribe, he promised Christ to convert to faith in him if Jesus would give him victory against the overwhelming forces of his enemy poised to destroy him. He won the battle; and in 496 CE (or soon thereafter) Clovis accepted baptism into the Christian church at the hands of Remigius, Bishop of Tours. He required his officers to accept baptism, as well.

Actually, though, Clovis merely changed religions without changing his gods. He still worshipped Woden and Thor, Germanic gods of war and bloodshed. Now, though, he merged them into one and called his new one god "Jesus Christ." We know he still served the German gods of war, because that's the way he lived. He had only half-converted. He was now a pagan "Christian"—or merely a half-Christian. His Merovingian dynasty would rule almost every nation in Europe for the next 200 years, constituting without a doubt the most vile, repulsive set of rulers ever to infect Europe.

Now, Clovis had a major problem among his Frankish warriors—blood-feuds. Each murder or accidental killing required the victim's family to avenge that death by killing either the killer or anyone in his family. He faced the medieval version of the Hatfields and McCoys. It does not require much imagination to realize this situation could decimate his army in short order. The king had to do something to preserve his fighting force.

Being of a quick and inventive mind, Clovis came up with a solution. A concept already existed within Frankish culture that he only had to write into law and enforce. That system was called *Weregild* (VER-GILT), German for man-price and meaning blood-money. Each person in Germanic society had a monetary value assigned to his personal worth, ranging from the minimal value of a free man, to the higher value of the nobility, on up to the supreme value of a member of the royalty. By the time of Clovis' death in 511, he had passed into law the code known as *Pactis Legis Salicae*.

Among its many provisions, that legal code stipulated that the only retaliation to be exacted for the death of a family member was the prescribed price within *Weregild*. A family could not avenge the death of a family member by killing the murderer or a member of his family or clan. They could only require that the murderer or accidental killer pay the man-price, the *Weregild*. "Christian" Clovis, himself a violent cruel man, had no difficulty enforcing his new law that stopped the interminable blood-feuds ravaging his people.

Clovis could not possibly have realized that with this act of giving legal force to an old Frankish and Germanic principle, he had laid a significant section of the road leading to a major theory of the atonement that would dominate Christian theology for a thousand years. The next section would be laid almost six hundred years later by a descendant of the Vikings, a French Duke who lusted after the crown of England.

William the Conqueror and Feudalism

The Franks after Clovis advanced and solidified into numerous Frankish states. In 876 the Viking Norseman Hrolf Gaanger invaded France. Charles the Simple, king of West Francia, bought off Hrolf by ceding to him the area now known as Normandy, named for those Norsemen. These Viking invaders accepted the Catholic religion, settled down, married local women, adopted the French language, and grew into good Frenchmen. In time they became the Dukes of Normandy. During their stay in France, the French economy and political system flowered into feudalism.

In 1066 a descendant of Hrolf crossed the English Channel and invaded England. At the Battle of Hastings, Duke William of Normandy defeated King Harold of England and assumed the English throne.[2] With the arrival of the Conqueror, England began to suffer under the rule of the Norman French nobility. William not only introduced into England the French language and rule, but also imported the feudalistic system already developed to some measure of completeness in France.

The story of King Arthur and his Roundtable centuries before William the Conqueror is pure fantasy. Actually, the Conqueror's grandson instigated the writing of that legend. Henry II commissioned Geoffrey of Monmouth to write a complete story of the Celtic warrior Arthur for the purpose of unifying the English people. It worked, and we love that story to this day; but the entire feudalistic panoply of English knights in armor actually began with William I, not King Arthur.

The feudalism imported from France consisted of a complex economic and political system based on land and military service.[3] A "lord" (king, duke, or earl) gave his "vassal" (military subordinate) a "fief" (land). This land might be a relatively small piece of property or a vast estate of thousands of acres including a castle and many towns and villages; however, the vassal did not actually own the land. He did not have "tenure" but only "possessed" it as long as he met the requirements of his liege lord.

In return for the fief, the vassal pledged to his lord "fealty" (loyalty) and "homage" (military service, from the French word *homme*, meaning "man"). Homage meant the vassal as the lord's "man" would serve him as a soldier in time of war. Faithfulness to the pledge was an entirely personal loyalty to the king or noble to whom a soldier was attached, not to the state. The lord in turn pledged the vassal his protection, occupation of his estate, employment, and usually wealth as long as he maintained fealty and homage. The vassal also owed his lord either to work the land himself or to oversee the working of the land by others, if it was a vast estate given to a duke or earl. From the proceeds of the land, the vassal owed his lord taxes as payment for the privilege of possessing the property.

The part of feudalism that interests us in this study, however, concerns what happened if the vassal failed or rebelled against his lord, that is, if he committed "treason." If a vassal offended his lord in any significant way, he owed him "satisfaction." By this time, feudalism had absorbed Clovis' concept of *Weregild*, not so much the word as the idea. Originally under Clovis, *Weregild* applied only to murder; but in time it came to apply to any failure or "treason," even adultery by the lord's wife. (Think of Henry VIII and Anne Boleyn.)

"Satisfaction" meant the compensation due one's lord for the loss he had incurred from the vassal's action or inaction. This compensation included what we would call today damages for actual loss incurred plus punitive damages. The satisfaction owed one's lord varied according to the rank of the lord. A major offense against a knight would merit one amount of satisfaction. An offense against a duke or earl would bring a much larger satisfaction. An offense against a king might demand one's own tortured death.

The true loss to any duke, earl, or king was damage to his "honor." The satisfaction required to cover loss of honor to a member of the nobility or royalty was high. During the feudal period such penalties as chopping off noses and ears, blinding, castration, beheading, burning alive, and drawing and quartering were common.

Drawing and quartering in "Christian" England involved hanging and simultaneous disemboweling the victim—while still alive—and then cutting the corpse into quarters and displaying the pieces in public places as a warning to other malefactors.

Like Clovis of the Franks almost six centuries before, William I of England could not have imagined that with the economic and political system he imported into England, he had paved another significant section of the road to a major theory of the atonement.

Lanfranc, William II, and Anselm

Lanfranc led troops in William the Conqueror's victory over England's King Harold. As his reward for military service, the Conqueror appointed him Archbishop of Canterbury. Lanfranc subsequently stood beside William as his most trusted friend and councilor. William I died in 1087 and his son William "Rufus" ascended the throne as William II, reigning from 1087 until 1100. Like Clovis and the Conqueror, William II played a critical role in the later development of the Christian doctrine of the atonement. His role came about in this fashion.

Two years after assuming the throne, Rufus found himself without his father's dearest councilor when Lanfranc died. The young king did not appoint a new archbishop for several years; instead, he appropriated the church's receipts to his own coffers. Eventually, when he decided to appoint an archbishop, he naturally looked back home to France for a successor to Lanfranc. On the other side of the English Channel, he spotted a brilliant Benedictine theologian whom he had earlier recruited as Abbot of Bec.

Henry craftily enticed the reluctant abbot to come to England for a visit, then forbade him to leave, and forcibly appointed him the new Archbishop of Canterbury. With this bold move, William II installed at Canterbury the leading Roman Catholic theologian in Europe at the time, Anselm of Bec. After that appointment, he was known as Anselm of Canterbury.[4]

William II had a stormy relationship with Archbishop Anselm. The king was a totally irreligious man, bereft of any morals other than loyalty to his troops. He had no culture aside from that of a soldier. Anselm complained on one occasion, "You would yoke an old sheep to an untamed bull."[5] The ruler and his archbishop were forever at odds with one another, falling out and reconciling only to fall out again.

On one occasion, Anselm found his life and liberty in danger in Canterbury when he fell into William Rufus' disfavor and fled to France for sanctuary. While biding his time until he could return to his post in England, he penned one of the more significant theological treatises ever written, *Cur Deus Homo*. Literally meaning "Why the God-Man," the title is usually translated "Why God Became Man."[6]

In this short treatise, the process that began with the semi-Christian Clovis 600 years earlier and advanced when William the Conqueror imported French feudalism into England came to its theological fruition.

The archbishop set out to explain why it was necessary for God to incarnate himself in Jesus of Nazareth and die on the cross for the salvation of the human race. This book—more than any other—has influenced the way the gospel of Jesus Christ has been preached ever since. Now more than nine hundred years later, the vast majority of conservative evangelical preachers when attempting to explain the atonement revert to some permutation of this medieval theory derived from feudal law with meager New Testament support. Few men have had such an extensive reach in the history of human thought.

Anselm derived his theory of the atonement from two strands of then current ideas: the Roman Catholic practice of penance and the medieval economic-political institution we now call "feudalism." We will look first at the minor partner in this duo, penance; then we will conclude with the major partner, feudalism.

Origins of Anselm's Satisfaction Theory of the Atonement

PENANCE
Post-baptismal sin demands satisfaction (compensation) to God.

FEUDALISM
A vassal's treason (offense) against his lord to whom he owes fealty and homage demands satisfaction (compensation) proportionate to the status of the lord (*Weregild*).

ANSELM'S SATISFACTION THEORY
Sin against infinite God demands infinite satisfaction.

Only a human can offer the satisfaction.

Only a divine person can provide it.

Thus, the God-Man offered himself as vicarious satisfaction for our sin-debt.

Satisfaction Theory and Penance

Near the turn of the third century, the Berber Christian Tertullian of Carthage (ca. 155–ca. 240) had introduced the concept of "satisfaction" into church theology.[7] Having been a lawyer, that North African churchman naturally thought in terms of sinful deeds demanding reparations or satisfaction. Others picked up and echoed Tertullian's idea. Tertullian and his imitators only meant that God demands satisfaction from us for post-baptismal sins. Thus was born the primitive doctrine of penance—from the Latin word *paenitentia* meaning repentance. In time the word penance possibly came to carry additionally some of the sense of the Latin word *poena*, meaning compensation, punishment, and pain.

At first a special repentance was required only for the serious sins after baptism, with idolatry, adultery, and murder being excluded from the possibility of penance. Penance and restoration to the church were available to a person only once in a lifetime. Usually, furthermore, penance was only imposed on churchmen or the nobility and royalty. As the practice of penance developed, however, it eventually came to include confession of all sin, repentance for sin, completion of certain actions to provide evidence of one's repentance, and pronouncement of absolution by the bishop (or later by a priest). By the third century, the word satisfaction came to be used in connection with penance and meant essentially the same thing as penance. Cyprian, Bishop of Carthage, for instance, in the early third century linked penance and satisfaction.[8]

Anselm's satisfaction theory of the atonement owed far more to another factor, however, than it did either to the writings of the church fathers or to the practice of penance.

Satisfaction Theory and Feudalism

In his preface to *Cur Deus Homo*, Anselm wrote a highly significant paragraph. Having stated that his work is divided into two "books," he goes on to say:

> The first [book] contains the objections of infidels, who despise the Christian faith because they deem it contrary to reason; and also the reply of believers; and in fine [in short], leaving Christ out of view (as if nothing had ever been known of him), it proves, by absolute reasons, the impossibility that any man should be saved without him. Again, in the second book, likewise, as if nothing were known of Christ, it is moreover shown by plain reasoning and fact that human nature was ordained for this purpose . . .[9]

In other words, the archbishop sets himself the task of proving from pure reason, without reference to the teachings or person of Jesus Christ, even without any reference to Scripture, that his theory of the atonement is necessarily true as a matter of logic.

Anselm's "pure reason" tells him that humanity has sinned against God and has thereby dishonored God and committed a major offense against God's "honor." God's "justice, which maintains God's honor,"[10] requires "that satisfaction or punishment must needs follow every sin" (derived from feudalism). Furthermore, the satisfaction owed to God "should be proportionate to guilt" (borrowed from the Frankish principle of *Weregild*). But everything the sinner could give God "to vindicate the honor of God" and "to restore what he owes to God" one already owes to God as Sovereign.[11] It becomes, therefore, impossible for sinful humans to restore to God his lost honor, lost through our sin, since anything we could do to serve God we already owe to God. For this reason, the Son of God became a man so that as sinless man he could repay on our behalf that massive debt owed God by humanity.

Anselm did not take his doctrine from Scripture or the teachings of Jesus and did not claim to do so. Neither did he develop his doctrine of the atonement from pure reason, which he did claim to do.[12] Remember that Anselm served as Archbishop of Canterbury in feudal England under the reign of a man whose father brought feudalism to England. At the time he wrote, he was hiding out in France where feudalism had been born and developed and where he had lived and served as an abbot before becoming Archbishop of Canterbury.

Anselm had lived most of his adult life under feudalism—either in the land of its birth or in the land of its transplantation. Furthermore, he had absorbed that mentality almost from birth, having been born into Lombard nobility. Anselm explained the atonement of Jesus Christ in the only language he knew—the language of feudalism—fealty and homage, lost honor, royal justice, debt, and satisfaction. No doubt, his explanation communicated powerfully to people similarly reared in that culture. He thought what he wrote was pure reason, but it actually represented pure cultural conditioning.

Today, we have two problems with Anselm's theory. First, Anselm's imagery does not speak to us. We no longer think in terms of wringing the last drop of vengeance from someone who has failed or dishonored us. We do not think in terms of fealty and homage, offense to our honor, or satisfaction for honor lost.

Second, and more important theologically, Anselm's explanation also stood contrary to Scripture and to the teachings and spirit of Jesus Christ. The archbishop had no idea how contrary to both Scripture and Jesus his theory ran. He had lived under feudalistic brutality so long he could not see what a horrifying picture of God it proclaimed.

Abba, *Father*

Most of us, however, do not know the satisfaction theory of the atonement as Anselm taught it. Most of us know it as John Calvin reshaped it—the penal substitution theory. For that reason, in the next chapter we will jump 400 years into the future to the early modern period to look at the teaching of the Reformer John Calvin of Geneva, Switzerland.

Notes

[1] The facts for this material are derived from many sources. The following online sources are typical: Yasmin Devi-McGleish and David J. Cox, *From Weregild to a Way Forward? English Restorative Justice in Its Historical Context*; Donald L. Wasson, "Clovis I," *Ancient History Encyclopedia*, 2014, www.ancient.eu/Clovis_I; Kathleen Mitchel, "Clovis I," *Encyclopedia Britannica*, www.britannica.com/biography/Clovis-I. For the Franks, *Weregild*, Clovis, and the Merovingians, see also Will Durant, *The Story of Civilization: The Age of Faith* (New York: Simon and Schuster, 1950), 88-94.

[2] See David Howarth, *1066: The Year of the Conquest* (Dorset Press, 1977).

[3] For more information on feudalism see Christopher Brooke, *From Alfred to Henry III: 871–1271* (New York: Norton, 1971), 94-105; Joseph and Frances Gies, *Life in a Medieval Castle* (New York: Perennial, 1974), 32-56; Will Durant, *Story of Civilization: The Age of Faith*, vol. 4 (New York: Simon and Schuster, 1950), 552-579; or Frank McLynn, *Richard and John: Kings at War* (Cambridge, MA.: DaCapo, 2007), 70, 85, 299, 323.

[4] For the relationship between William II and Anslem see Brooke, *From Alfred to Henry III*, 153-159.

[5] Brooke, Ibid., 157.

[6] Anselm, *Cur Deus Homo: Why God Became Man*, trans. Sidney Norton Deane (Pantianos Classics, 1903, 2016).

[7] J.N.D. Kelly, *Early Christian Doctrines* (New York: Harper and Row, 1960), 177.

[8] *The Ante-Nicene Fathers*, ed. Alexander Roberts and James Donaldson, vol. 5, *Fathers of the Third Century, Cyprian*, pp. 267-596. Epistles 28, 52, pp. 306, 336. Also *The Fathers of the Church: Saint Cyprian, Treatises*, ed. and trans. Roy Joseph Deferrari (New York: Fathers of the Church, Inc., 1958), pp. 69-72, 82, 84-88. See also Oscar Daniel Watkins, *A History of Penance* (London: Longmans, Green and Co., 1920), 214. For the development of penance and "satisfaction," see Oscar Daniel Watkins, *A History of Penance, Being A Study of Authorities (a) For the Whole Church to A.D. 450, (b) For the Western Church from A.D. 450 to A.D. 1215*, in 2 volumes (London: Longmans, Green and Co., 1920). Also, see Sarah Hamilton, *The Practice of Penance, 900-1050* (London: Boydell, 2001).

[9] Anselm, Ibid.,vi.

[10] Anselm, Ibid., 6. Also 41, 48, 49, 50. This idea recurs repeatedly throughout the book.

[11] Ibid., 27, 29, 40, 43, 45.

[12] Charles Hefling has provided a brilliant refutation—from "pure reason," if you will—of Anselm's theory in "Why the Cross? God's At-One-Ment with Humanity," *The Christian Century*, March 11, 2013.

Chapter 9

Calvin's Penal Substitution Theory

John Calvin reworded Anselm's theory of the atonement to say that because we have sinned, God is hostile to us; and only through the substitutionary death of Christ can God be propitiated and enabled to forgive us.

John Calvin

Four centuries after Anselm wrote *Cur Deus Homo* in France, Jean Cauvin was born into the Roman Catholic church in that same country. In his early life he studied law and intended to pursue a career in that profession. In his twenties he turned to the new Protestant movement begun earlier by Martin Luther. In time he ended up in Geneva, Switzerland, where he made his name and established his enduring legacy. By this time, he had changed his last name to Calvin.

In 1536, at the age of 27, he published in Latin the first edition of his *magnum opus Institutes of the Christian Religion*. This work went through several editions and translations into French before Calvin published his fourth massive edition in 1559. This edition, the one we know today as Calvin's *Institutes*, ran a thousand pages.[1]

Calvin's monumental book shaped the Huguenots of France, the Dutch Reformed of the Netherlands, the Puritans of England, and the Presbyterians of Scotland and the United States.[2] Calvin's *Institutes* has left an enduring theological influence in the Christian world. For Reformed churches, it is the foundational interpretation of the Bible on everything from church government, to theology, to the sacraments. Possibly the most famous of Calvin's teachings among non-Reformed believers is his doctrine of election and predestination. Whether Reformed or not, however, a broad swath of the Protestant world has absorbed Calvin's understanding of the atonement—how the death of Jesus Christ provides salvation to a fallen race. That doctrine will occupy our attention in this chapter.

Calvin on the Atonement

When still in his twenties Calvin began to attempt to understand how Jesus brought salvation to the human race. He had ready at hand a number of theories of the atonement from which to choose. Of course, Anselm's then 400-year-old satisfaction theory stood front and center.

The archbishop had seen the difficulty in reconciling humanity and God as a problem for God. His model went like this: Since our Judge is just, he cannot overlook any diminution of his honor and, therefore, absolutely must punish sin. Our Creator, however, is also loving, and desires to forgive the sinner. Thus, God finds a tension, a conflict, within himself. He, therefore, incarnated his Son in Jesus of Nazareth. Being a man, Jesus could pay man's sin debt; being deity, he did not owe any sin debt already. Therefore, the God-Man could provide the atonement by paying God in humanity's stead the satisfaction we owe him.

Other models did exist, though. For example, about three hundred years before Calvin, the Roman Catholic theologian Thomas Aquinas had developed an alternative concept to Anselm's. Aquinas, by contrast to Anselm, saw the problem with atonement as belonging to humanity: The human will is infected with sin and therefore does not and cannot will to do God's will. Christ's death provides "the grace that heals the defect in the human will through the processes of justification and sanctification."[3]

Alternatively, Calvin could have chosen the ransom theory—the idea that Christ's death bought the freedom of humanity by paying a ransom to the devil. That explanation had been around for centuries, going back to Irenaeus in the second century.[4] Calvin read widely in the early church fathers, so he could have adopted any of the many explanations of the atonement offered through the centuries.[5]

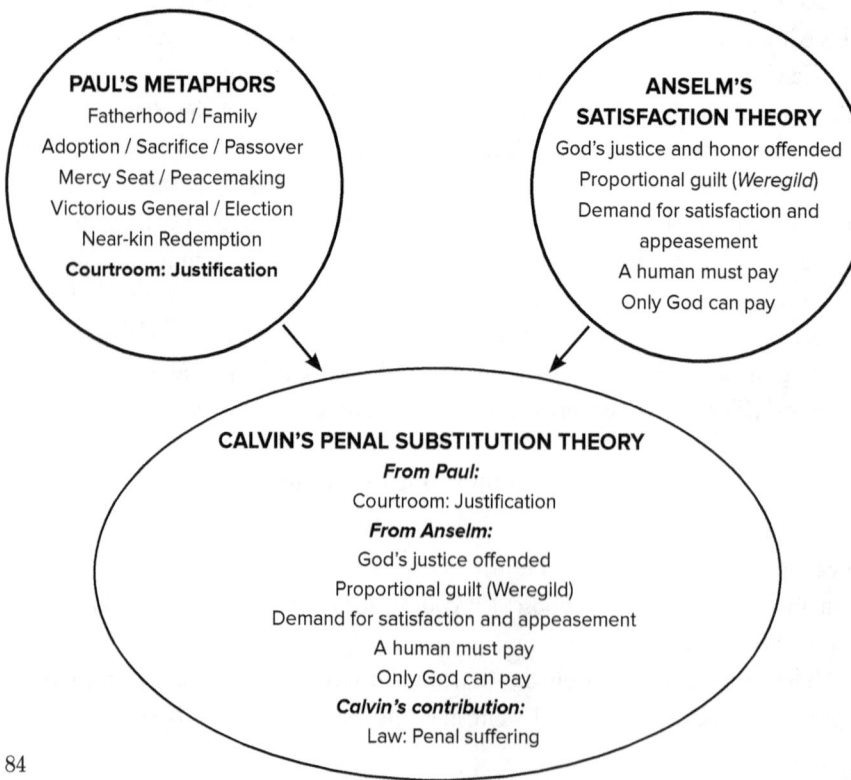

Sources of Calvin's Penal Substitution Theory

PAUL'S METAPHORS
Fatherhood / Family
Adoption / Sacrifice / Passover
Mercy Seat / Peacemaking
Victorious General / Election
Near-kin Redemption
Courtroom: Justification

ANSELM'S SATISFACTION THEORY
God's justice and honor offended
Proportional guilt (*Weregild*)
Demand for satisfaction and appeasement
A human must pay
Only God can pay

CALVIN'S PENAL SUBSTITUTION THEORY
From Paul:
Courtroom: Justification
From Anselm:
God's justice offended
Proportional guilt (Weregild)
Demand for satisfaction and appeasement
A human must pay
Only God can pay
Calvin's contribution:
Law: Penal suffering

Calvin found himself drawn to the satisfaction theory of Anselm, which he adopted and adapted. Possibly Calvin's training as a lawyer had a great deal to do with his adapting Anselm's theory. The Reformer found in Galatians and Romans the courtroom metaphor of justification. It seems likely Calvin combined his prior legal training with Paul's forensic picture of justification and Anselm's legalistic satisfaction theory. The feudal metaphor of satisfaction, however, no longer resonated by the sixteenth century. He, therefore, modified that image to Paul's courtroom metaphor and came up with the demand for penal suffering. Thus was born Calvin's theory of the atonement.

Although Anselm's satisfaction theory and Calvin's penal substitution theory have two different names, they are actually different versions of the same doctrine. The changes Calvin made to Anselm's satisfaction theory amounted to a distinction without a difference.

Penal Substitution Theory

IDEA	GUILT	MEANING
Proportional guilt	FRANKISH TRADITION Guilt proportional to person offended (from *Weregild*)	Since God is infinite, our guilt against him is infinite, which we as finite creatures cannot pay
Satisfaction Theory	ANSELM Against God's honor and justice (from feudalism)	Jesus' death paid satisfaction for the offense of our sins to God's honor (or justice).
Penal Substitution Theory	JOHN CALVIN Against God's justice	Jesus' death paid our debt for the offense of our sins to God's justice.
Sin debt idea	TODAY Guilt debt against God's holiness or righteousness	Jesus' death paid our sin debt for the offense of our sins to God's holiness or righteousness.

Penal Substitution

In Adam's sin, Calvin insisted, all humans sinned.[6] Because of our sin in Adam, we all owe God a debt.[7] Until this debt is paid, God remains our "enemy" and we lie under the "wrath" of God. God's "vengeance" and "eternal death" are our lot. Our sin debt must be paid as a "penalty" owed to God "to satisfy God's justice." Jesus died as a "sacrifice," a "substitute," dying the death we owed to God, in order to pay that debt and to "satisfy God's justice."[8] In dying on the cross "to pay the price of our redemption" and to "satisfy the justice of God," Jesus Christ became our "Redeemer."[9] He "purchased life for us."

This brief paragraph condenses and paraphrases Calvin's fifty pages setting forth his understanding of the biblical teaching on the atonement wrought by Jesus Christ.[10] In addition to satisfaction, another major concept of Calvin's recurs again and again that is central to his penal substitution theory: propitiation.

Propitiating God

"Propitiation" sounds odd to the ordinary person not steeped in conservative Christian theology. This strange word almost no one uses anymore has a simple meaning. If a person displays kindness to another, she is *propitious* toward that person. If a person changes the mind of an enemy by doing something he appreciates, then he is said to *propitiate* him. That is, he changes the enemy's mind from being angry with himself to feeling *propitious* toward him. *Appease* and *placate* carry similar connotations. Calvin said the work of Jesus Christ as our Mediator is "to restore us to the divine favor" and "to appease the just anger of his Father." He also said that Jesus "made a propitiation for us" and propitiated "the Father to us by becoming a victim."[11]

Because "God in his character of judge is hostile to us" and "could not be propitiated without the expiation of sin," Christ "by the sacrifice of his death … wiped away our guilt, and made satisfaction for sin."[12] In other words, because we have sinned, God is hostile to us; he is our "enemy" and could not possibly be otherwise, because of his "justice." Only through the substitutionary death of Christ—literally, in our place—can God be "propitiated," made friendly toward us and enabled to forgive us.

Calvin's Problem

Calvin himself recognized a problem in this theology, a difficulty he mentioned in the following paragraph.

> But before we proceed farther, we must see in passing, how can it be said that God, who prevents [precedes] us with his mercy, was our enemy until he was reconciled to us by Christ. For how could he have given us in his only begotten Son a singular pledge of his love, if he had not previously embraced us with free favor? As there thus arises some *appearance of contradiction*, I will explain the difficulty.[13] [author's italics]

In spite of what Calvin says here, the problem and the contradiction are real, far more than the mere appearance he thinks. Calvin then proceeds to explain the difficulty by saying the problem lies in God's adapting himself to our weakness. "Such modes of expression are accommodated to our capacity." In other words, God speaks to us in metaphors.

Exactly!

Unfortunately, Calvin did not realize that he had made the deadly interpretive mistake of taking the metaphors of Scripture literally. He attempted to build a semi-philosophical theology of the atonement on a literal understanding of words that cannot be taken literally—by his own admission.

Evaluating Calvin's Theology

John Calvin, like all the sixteenth-century Reformers, presents the twenty-first-century believer with a bag of contradictions. He was truly a great man, Christian, theologian, and biblical interpreter. He did the nearly impossible. He critiqued the religious ideas in which he had been reared and indoctrinated, ideas intuitively accepted by everyone he knew—and paid a high price for it. In departing from Roman Catholic theology (although only partially), he alienated himself from his friends, church, government, and nation. He had to flee his home country and make his way to a foreign land. Few people can face such overwhelming loss to follow their vision of truth.

Yet, Calvin lived in the early years of the Reformation's return to Scripture. He and his fellow Reformers would develop the rubric of "Scripture alone, Christ alone, grace alone, and faith alone." They were just beginning to understand what the Bible and Jesus taught concerning God's nature and atonement, however, not finishing with a perfected product.

Now, half a millennium after the Reformers, we stand on the shoulders of twenty to twenty-five generations of biblical scholars, theologians, and historians who followed in their train. No one could reasonably expect those gigantic seminal thinkers to arrive in a single generation at the insights we should have five centuries later. Furthermore, even after half a millennium of interpreting the Scriptures according to the principles they laid down, we are still struggling with many of these same concepts.

In spite of the faulty doctrine of the atonement taught by Calvin, he still grasped something of the wonderful revelation of God's love revealed and bestowed in Jesus of Nazareth. We owe a great debt of gratitude to him and the other Reformers for plowing new ground and allowing us to follow them in the task of delving into the Scriptures to understand the mind of Christ.

Calvin's teachers in the church from antiquity, however, had conveyed to him such confusion in understanding the Scriptures, the gospel, and Jesus Christ, that

Abba, *Father*

we cannot fault him over much if he failed to rise above them entirely. Even today, author after author struggles to explain the atonement, trying desperately to find some way to explain Christ's "satisfaction," to explain how he paid our "sin debt," or to explain a change the cross produced in God.

From Clovis to Calvin

	Franks	**FRANKISH TRIBES** (by 5th century)	In *Weregild*, killing of relative demands proportionate compensation
	King of Franks	**CLOVIS** (496–511)	Made *Weregild* law in *Pactis Legis Salicae*
	Franks	**FRANKISH STATES** (486–987)	Absorbed *Weregild*
	French	**FEUDALISM** (by late 1000s)	Added concept of satisfaction
	Norman French	**WILLIAM I, King of England** (1066–1087)	Imported feudalism to England
	Norman French	**WILLIAM II, King of England** (1087–1100)	Brought Anselm to England from France
	Abbot of French Monastery	**ANSELM, Archbishop of Canterbury** (1093–1109)	Taught satisfaction theory in *Cur Deus Homo*
	French	**JOHN CALVIN**[14], **Geneva Minister** (1509–1564)	Taught penal substitution theory in *The Institutes*

With all due deference to one of the great pioneers of the Reformation, we can draw an almost straight line from the pagan Frankish king Clovis, through the early Frankish kingdoms, to the Frenchmen William Duke of Normandy and his son William II, to Anselm, Abbot of a French monastery, and ultimately to the Frenchman Calvin. They were all either Franks, French, or an abbot of a French monastery. To put it another way, we can almost draw a straight line from Frankish *Weregild* to French feudalism to a French monastery to the satisfaction theory to the penal substitution theory of the Frenchman John Calvin.

This favorite way of explaining the gospel has nothing to do with Scripture or the teachings of Jesus Christ. It has everything to do with medieval Frankish and French culture. It seems that once an idea gets "out there," however, everyone who comes afterward feels compelled to honor it. Once Anselm placed the word "satisfaction" and the idea of a "sin debt" into theological currency, few dared challenge it.

Notes

[1] John Calvin, *Institutes of the Christian Religion*, trans. Henry Beveridge. (Peabody, MA: Hendrikson, 2008), xv.

[2] Ibid., xiv.

[3] Eleanor Stumpf, *Atonement* (Oxford: Oxford, 2018), 23.

[4] Irenaeus, *Against Heresies*, Book V.I.1, A. Cleveland Coxe, *The Apostolic Fathers*, I (Grand Rapids: Eerdmans, 1969), 527.

[5] See J.N.D. Kelly, *Early Christian Doctrines* (New York: Harper and Row, 1960), Chapter XIV: Christ's Saving Work, 375-400.

[6] Calvin, Ibid., 150-151.

[7] The following material is extracted from Ibid., 298-299, 322, 325, 328-329, 341,599.

[8] Placing key words in quotation marks indicates that these words actually appear in Calvin's dissertation; they are not this author's creation as a paraphrase or a caricature of what he said. Calvin actually said it this way, just as many preachers phrase it today.

[9] Notice that Calvin misidentified our Redeemer.

[10] Calvin, Ibid., Book Second, Chapters 12-17, 297-343.

[11] Ibid., 298, 299, 300.

[12] Ibid., 322.

[13] Ibid., 325.

[14] Martin Luther had arrived at the same conception of the atonement prior to Calvin. Nevertheless, Luther also stood in a similar direct spiritual "line of descent" from the Germanic concept of *Weregild* and Anselm's satisfaction theory in arriving at his penal substitution theory of the atonement.

Chapter 10

Penal Substitution Today

Calvin's penal substitution theory still appears essentially unchanged in many conservative Christian pulpits and books and frequently finds scholarly defense.

Calvin's Theory as We Hear It Preached Today

As the church comes to receive the Sunday morning offering, the pastor calls on a deacon to lead in prayer. That deacon intones, "O God, we thank you that you sent your son to earth to die for us and pay our sin-debt to make it possible for you to forgive us of our sins." Then the pastor proclaims in his sermon, "You have sinned against God. Our God is an infinite God. Therefore, sin against our infinite God carries an infinite guilt. But we are finite creatures and cannot possibly pay an infinite debt. For this reason, the Son of God had to become a man so that as man he could pay our infinite sin debt, making it possible for God to forgive us of our sins and take us to live with him in heaven."

Fifteen hundred years after the Frankish king Clovis, that deacon and pastor have stated the gospel in terms of pagan Germanic *Weregild*. God as the ultimate feudal lord demands the ultimate man-price, which only the Son of God incarnate in Jesus of Nazareth can pay. Nine hundred years after Anselm of Canterbury, many American Christians still express the Good News of what Jesus did for us in terms of paying God satisfaction for having violated his righteousness or his holiness (whichever word an individual pastor prefers). Almost no one speaks today of having deprived God of "honor," Anselm's word, but many of us still use the language of Calvin from half a millennium ago.

Whenever you hear a preacher speak of "the wrath of holy God against sin," he frequently speaks out of the same set of theological doctrines. We have offended God and some human being must pay the price before God can forgive us. To forgive us without the payment of "satisfaction" would violate God's justice, or holiness, or righteousness. We cannot pay the satisfaction, so God's Son incarnated (embodied) in Jesus of Nazareth paid the sin-debt we could not pay. Only then could God forgive our sins and save us and take us to heaven to enjoy him forever.

Current Defenses of Penal Substitution

Much conservative preaching of the cross of Christ presents the penal substitution theory of the atonement in highly objectionable ways. Such preaching implies that God requires someone to pay the price for our sin before he will forgive us and accept us as his children. In this presentation, Jesus' death on the cross paid the infinite "sin debt" we owe to God and makes it possible for God to forgive us.

The best of conservative writers, however, defend the penal substitution without many of the most objectionable features of some popular preaching. Leon Morris,[1] James I. Packer,[2] and John R.W. Stott[3] serve as examples of informed, scholarly defenders of the penal substitution theory. (Others have been mentioned in passing in endnotes and appear in appendices of this work.)

John Stott's book *The Cross of Christ* possibly represents the best of these defenses. Stott recognizes the objectionable elements of many versions of this theory and labors valiantly to remove them. He does so effectively for the most part, presenting a reasonable, courteous, and scholarly understanding of penal substitution. Much of his presentation of penal substitution rings compatible with the view presented in this work, especially his emphasis on God as the Father who saves us. He insists that no one, not even Christ, had to appease an angry God to induce him to move from enmity to friendship. His view that in the cross God himself offers the means to our forgiveness is attractive. At the same time, Stott retains several concepts that display the fatal flaws in the penal substitution theory of the atonement.

The Tension in God

The key terminal mistake in penal substitution resides in the concept of the tension within God that presents him as finding a difficulty within himself in forgiving sinners. God's love leads God to desire to forgive his children, but his justice demands that his wrath against sin punish all sinners and demand reparations. Stott actually raises the question as he addresses a point raised a century ago by an earlier theologian. "Was P.T. Forsyth correct in writing that 'there is nothing in the Bible about the strife of attributes?'" he asks. To which he replies, "I do not think he was." He then cites a passage from Hosea and concludes, "Here surely is a conflict of emotions, a strife of attributes, within God."[4] He proceeds to quote Packer approvingly that Jesus "endured and exhausted the destructive divine judgment for which we were otherwise inescapably destined."[5]

My objection to this kind of theologizing lies in the fact that nowhere in the teaching of Jesus do we find any such divine quandary puzzling over how the Father will solve his problem. Our Lord proclaimed God simply as the loving Father who delights to give good things to his children, who delights to forgive the repentant.

Jesus himself commanded us to "Be merciful, just as your Father is merciful" (Luke 6:36). The very idea of God struggling with an internal dilemma among his own attributes appears odd indeed. Such a concept of God does not jibe with Jesus' proclamation of his loving *Abba*.

Confusing Sacrifice and Punishment[6]

Stott, like Morris and Packer, engages in nearly exhaustive examination of biblical texts in his search to ascertain what Scripture teaches about the atonement. He builds a case that leaves the impression that he has exegeted every conceivable text on the subject, giving us no choice but to agree with his conclusions. A critical consideration of his texts, however, shows that most of his arguments center around three kinds of texts: those on sacrifice, those suggesting substitution, and those using a certain vocabulary they take as implying propitiation. Let's begin by thinking about the texts on sacrifice before we move one at a time to the others.

Stott zeroes in on one unquestionable emphasis of the New Testament discussion of the significance of Jesus of Nazareth and his crucified death. Almost every author in the New Testament speaks of the death of Jesus in terms of sacrifice—Passover, the Day of Atonement, or simply sacrifice in general. That point cannot be disputed.

The question, however, remains: "What does the metaphor of sacrifice signify?" Stott seems to take the metaphor literally. A literal understanding of sacrifice in connection with the cross, though, is not possible. Nothing about the death of Jesus—the location, the manner, the method, the executor—corresponds to a literal sacrifice of a lamb or a bull by priests on the altar in the Jerusalem Temple complex. Obviously, the sacrifice motif is a metaphor. In that case, a metaphor of what?

I find nothing in the teaching of Jesus about his own death to suggest that he considered his ensuing crucifixion to represent any sort of judicial verdict of vicarious punishment exacted by his Father. Then what? It seems obvious that the metaphor of sacrifice represents the exceedingly costly nature of God's forgiveness and redemption—rescue—of his children. Stott insists that God redeems us in his Son. Stott's presentation of the Father as sacrificing himself in his Son for our salvation appears to remove some of the offensive nature of penal substitution.

Having acknowledged these points, he does not adequately justify positing a need for God to exact a punishment to be endured—not even by himself in the person of his embodiment in Jesus—to make his forgiveness possible. The illogical jump from the picture of sacrifice to that of judicial punishment seems wholly unnecessary. The Father in Jesus' preaching simply calls us to himself and pursues us all the way to the cross to bring us home. Self-sacrifice does not imply punishment judicially exacted.

Abba, *Father*

Confusing Substitution and Penal Judgment[7]

The second set of texts on which Stott and others focus are those texts suggesting that somehow God's forgiveness bestowed in Jesus Christ is substitutionary. Again, while many interpreters have attempted to deny this implication in these texts, such denial rings implausible. God's offer of reconciliation with humanity does seem to contain a distinct element of substitution.

Moreover, *all* forgiveness whatever—by anyone—is substitutionary. The injured party refuses to pour his revenge on the head of the offender, accepts into himself the pain of the offense, and forgives it. In other words, in forgiveness the one forgiving *always* substitutes his own pain for the pain he could displace onto the other in seeking either reparations (satisfaction) or revenge. Such forgiveness does not mean the offense does not matter. If it did not matter, there would be no need for forgiveness. Such forgiveness does not mean that the injured party simply overlooks the offense. It means the injured person accepts the deep injury to himself without retaliating. This kind of forgiveness is grace, not apathy. It is substitutionary, but not penal.

I see two errors in Stott's approach at this point. He misunderstands the nature of forgiveness. He seems to think grace without satisfaction means treating the offense as unimportant or simply overlooking it. Forgiveness, however, becomes necessary only when the offense holds genuine significance. He also confuses the substitution element in forgiveness with punishment. He fails to recognize that self-sacrificing grace foregoes punishment. For all the positive aspects of Stott's presentation, his insistence that God must exact a penal demand for reparations for every offense against himself and punishment on the sinner remains objectionable. It seems he has once again leaped to an unnecessary conclusion reached rationalistically from an idea not taught either by Jesus Christ or the New Testament as a whole.

Faulty Linguistic Studies

The third mistake, it seems to me, made by these authors lies in the great weight they place on one particular Greek word-group that they understand to teach the doctrine of propitiation.[8] They all cite the same five texts in support of their doctrine. They always fail to point out that these are the only texts in the entire New Testament (plus one other not relevant to their argument) that contain the three different Greek words they interpret as meaning "propitiation." (For a more complete discussion of these words, see in chapter 6: "Propitiation in the Septuagint and New Testament" and endnotes 2, 3, 4, and 5 that deal with this vocabulary at some length.)

They also fail to discuss, curiously, how those words are used in the Septuagint, that these terms have highly different uses in the Septuagint than they impose on them in the New Testament, and that those words do not clearly contain the needed meaning in the New Testament. Then, by virtue of what they fail to point out about the rarely used word and its kin, they induce the reader to think their conclusion is inescapable. Most readers, having no familiarity with either the Hebrew text of Scripture or the Greek Septuagint, find themselves helpless to evaluate this line of argument. Actually, their argument contains far less than meets the eye.

The first of the three critical words, *hilasterion*,[9] never translates a Hebrew word meaning "propitiation" in the Septuagint. In those Scriptures of early Christians, this word invariably means either the Mercy Seat (the overwhelming majority of the time), the ledge around the Altar of the Temple (three times), or the capital of a column in the Temple (once). In Hebrews 9:5 almost all translations render it "Mercy Seat." Furthermore, in Romans 3:25 it almost certainly describes Jesus Christ metaphorically as our Mercy Seat—the place God has provided where our reconciliation to the Father takes place.

The second word, *hilaskomai*,[10] also occurs only twice in the New Testament. In Jesus' parable of the pharisee and the publican it means "be merciful" (Luke 18:13). In Hebrews 2:17 most translations render it "make a sacrifice of atonement" (as in the NRSV). Again, this word almost certainly means "forgive" or "cover" in Hebrews, as it does in all but one instance in the Septuagint. (The one exception is Exod. 32:14 where this word says God "repented.")

Leon Morris has argued that this word in Hebrews means "make propitiation,"[11] and numerous scholars have been led astray by his faulty analysis.[12] Morris and others holding to penal substitution fail to notice the difference in the way the Septuagint uses two similar but distinct words.[13] Through this failure to notice the different ways two distinct words are used, they equate them, when the Septuagint decidedly does not.

The third word, *hilasmos*,[14] occurs only in 1 John 2:2 and 4:10. If we let Septuagint usage guide us, we see that here this term means either a "sin offering"[15] or a "sacrifice of atonement."[16] Each of these three words occurs only twice in the New Testament and thus hardly represents a major New Testament theme. None of them clearly means "propitiation," although we can read that meaning into these verses if we have decided in advance to do so. All of these words were used very differently in the Greek Scriptures of the early church. In short, there is little historical reason to understand any of these three words so emphasized by the defenders of penal substitution as meaning propitiation.

Then why do these scholars and theologians interpret these five verses as they do? Why do they also interpret New Testament references to sacrifice and substitution as they do?

Begging the Question

They all begin, it seems to me, by presupposing the validity of the penal substitution theory of the atonement. This traditional interpretation has been around for five hundred years, and these interpreters find themselves incapable of doubting it for a moment. For example, Packer states early in his article, "Christians have from the start lived by faith in Christ's death as a sacrifice made to God in reparations for their sins."[17] But that is precisely the point that needs to be demonstrated, not presupposed. Notice that Packer's word "reparations" amounts to the equivalent of Anselm's "satisfaction" paid to God. Although defending Calvin's penal substitution theory, Packer is actually still bogged down in Anselm's satisfaction theory. This statement serves as his absolute presupposition for the remainder of his article. He fails to notice that what has been true for many for the past five centuries is hardly what has been true for all for the past two millennia, or what was true for Jesus and the New Testament authors.

Then, on the basis of that presupposition, these scholars read that idea into every verse of the New Testament referring to Jesus' death under the metaphor of sacrifice.[18] All other representations of the cross—the conquering Christ, the Mercy Seat, new birth, adoption, redemption (rescue), and so on—they read as metaphors, as they should. Whenever they encounter the metaphor of sacrifice, however, drawn from Jesus' and New Testament authors' experience of the Temple, they insist we take that metaphor literally. When critiqued concerning the problematic views of God their view entails, they retreat into comments concerning the limitations of metaphorical language. Having dealt with the critique, however, they immediately revert to taking this biblical metaphor literally. They make the same mistake Calvin made 500 years ago—taking literally what is actually metaphorical.

In spite of his efforts to remove the offense of penal substitution, Stott insists on retaining it all, albeit in a somewhat attenuated form. He insists on Calvin's key words and on Anselm's: satisfaction,[19] propitiation,[20] appease and placate,[21] curse,[22] penalty and punishment,[23] God's enmity and hostility.[24] Having presupposed the truth of penal substitution, he cannot give up a single point of it in spite of himself.

In short, Stott and company commit the deadly logical fallacy of "begging the question." They use their presupposition of the truth of the proposition under discussion to *prove* the truth of that proposition.[25] Having presupposed the truth of penal substitution, they read it into the New Testament everywhere. We also know this fallacy as the "vicious logical circle." This fallacy appears frequently in ordinary arguments of voters about politics or economics. We can explain this error in eminent scholars and theologians, though, only by remembering that these men are heirs to five centuries of tradition. The tradition holds such power for them, and they so implicitly assume its truth, that they see it constantly, even when historical and biblical precedent should lead them to different conclusions. We all live as creatures of our own cultures and cultural traditions.

The Solution

The first step in countering this theology is to recognize the various weaknesses of the defense of penal substitution—begging the question, reading meanings into Scripture that are not there, and highly questionable linguistic arguments. The second step moves as John MacQuarrie did long ago in his masterful book *God-Talk*[26] and recognizes that all our talk about God is metaphorical. God occupies a totally different sphere of being from us, so we know nothing about him that can be called literal. We have to speak of our experience of God metaphorically in order to say anything about him. The third step takes the time to ascertain *what Jesus said* relevant to the subject—that he presented God under the metaphor of our loving Father. The fourth step then interprets all the other metaphors—including sacrifice—consistently with our Lord's overarching metaphor.

When we take these steps, the ethical and spiritual problems disappear from New Testament teaching on atonement; and the Good News of Jesus Christ shines forth in all its simple beauty. No longer do we find ourselves under the necessity of defending the goodness and justice of God because of our faulty theology of atonement. We can simply rest in the confidence that God our loving Father has pursued us, his prodigal children, all the way to a tortured crucified death to bring us back into his fellowship. He forgives our murder of his Son, calls us to return to him, and welcomes us with a bear hug and a heavenly party when we come home. Then our fellowship with the Father in the power of his Spirit transforms our lives, and through us he transforms our world.

Theory on Top of Theory

For the last nine hundred years since Anselm and five hundred years since Calvin, Christian theologians have struggled to explain the atonement of Jesus Christ, burdened by the obligation to state that great reality in words at least somewhat reminiscent of the hallowed church tradition. That tradition begun with Archbishop Anselm and altered negligibly by the Reformer John Calvin has come down to us only slightly reworded. The greatest theologians of the past 500 years have struggled to restate it and remove its offensive elements.

Anselm and Calvin insisted, by implication, that Christ offered himself as our substitute for our sinfulness. In service of this idea, Scottish Reformed minister John McLeod Campbell (1800–1872) said that Jesus repented on behalf of the human race. In that vicarious repentance, he was our "substitute" (Calvin's word).[27]

English Congregationalist pastor P.T. Forsyth (1848–1921) said that Christ offered God a perfect obedience on our behalf. "Christ's judgment has objective value to the honour of God's holiness," Forsyth wrote. "He turned the penalty He endured into sacrifice He offered. And the sacrifice He offered was the judgment He accepted. His passive suffering became active obedience, and obedience to a holy doom."[28] Although he held a somewhat different concept of the atonement, Forsyth still felt constrained to use Anselm's word "honour" and Calvin's words "penalty" and "sacrifice." Forsyth still sounded a lot like Anselm and Calvin whom he could not resist imitating in spite of himself.

Hastings Rashdall (1858–1924) totally rejected Calvin's theology and presented the cross as a moral influence.[29] Christ's example calls us to a higher way of living. Don S. Browning, in contrast to the old traditional theology, saw the cross in terms of psychotherapy—that Christ heals our broken psyches.[30] Gustaf Aulen (1879–1977), adhering to New Testament terminology, presented the atonement under the rubric of Jesus Christ the conquering warrior who effects reconciliation of humanity to God.[31]

A number of recent theologians and biblical scholars have written on the atonement in imagery that more accurately reflects the thinking of Jesus Christ. Sixty years ago Anders Nygren saw the atonement as consisting of God graciously giving himself in love, willing to fellowship with humanity.[32] A few years later Fisher Humphreys presented a thrilling view of the atonement in terms of "cruciform forgiveness."[33] More recently, Stephen Finlan has described the preaching of Jesus as focused on the family metaphor of God the loving, forgiving Father.[34] He rejects the category of "atonement" entirely as embodying all the problematic features of the Christian history of the doctrine of atonement described here. His solution has much to commend it, although I have chosen to retain the word albeit redefined as "reconciliation."

Notes

[1] Leon Morris, *The Apostolic Preaching of the Cross* (Grand Rapids: Eerdmans, 1956).

[2] James I. Packer, "What Did the Cross Accomplish? The Logic of Penal Substitution" *Tyndale Bulletin*, vol. 25, 1974.

[3] John R.W. Stott, *The Cross of Christ* (Downers Grove, IL: IVP, 2006).

[4] Ibid., 129-130. See also on 179, among many examples.

[5] Stott, *The Cross of Christ*, 143; Packer, "What Did the Cross Accomplish?" 9, 25,29.

[6] Stott, *The Cross of Christ*, 74, 81. See also Packer, "What Did the Cross Accomplish?" 24.

[7] Stott, *The Cross of Christ*, 140-141, 143, 147, 199. See Packer, "What Did the Cross Accomplish?" 16ff.

[8] The Greek word ἱλασκομαι (*hilaskomai*) and related words.

[9] ἱλαστηριον (*hilasterion*).

[10] ἱλασκομαι (*hilaskomai*).

[11] Morris, *Apostolic Preaching*, 125, based on his confusion of ἱλασκομαι (*hilaskomai*) and ἐξιλασκομαι (*exilaskomai*), in spite of his lengthy discussion of the differences between these two words, 138ff.

Exilaskomai appears more than 100 times in the Septuagint, usually translating the Hebrew word-group *kipper*, and usually meaning either propitiation, expiation, or cleanse. *Hilaskomai* rarely appears in the Septuagint, and only once does it *possibly* mean propitiation. The defenders of penal substitution always equate the two words because of their similarity and fail to make the necessary distinction between them. *Hilaskomai* simply does not equal *exilaskomai*, which *never* appears in the New Testament.

¹²For example, William L. Lane, *Word Biblical Commentary: Hebrews 1–8* (Dallas: Word, 1991), 66, who quotes Packer approvingly.

¹³Stott, *The Cross of Christ*, 169, even argues that 1 Clement and the *Shepherd of Hermas* use *hilaskomai* to mean propitiation, but actually the word these two works used was *exilaskomai*. Stott's error here is compounded many times over by scholars who should have noticed the difference between these two words in the Septuagint. See Kittel, *Theological Dictionary of the New Testament*, III, 302, 314 fn 67, 315-316.

¹⁴ἱλασμος (*hilasmos*).

¹⁵As in Amos 8:14.

¹⁶As in Lev. 25:9 and Ezek. 44:27.

¹⁷Packer, "What Did the Cross Accomplish?" 9.

¹⁸As Packer does, Ibid., 31.

¹⁹Stott, *The Cross of Christ*, 117, 126. See also Packer, "What Did the Cross Accomplish?" 9, 21.

²⁰Stott, *The Cross of Christ*, 166-173, 194. See also Packer, "What Did the Cross Accomplish?" 10, 20-24, 38; Morris, Ibid., 125ff, 161ff.

²¹Stott, *The Cross of Christ*, 179. See also Morris, *Apostolic Preaching*, 126, 153.

²²Stott, *The Cross of Christ*, 81.

²³Ibid., 147. See also Packer, "What Did the Cross Accomplish?" 4, 21, 25ff, 29; Morris, *Apostolic Preaching*, 185, 232.

²⁴Stott, *The Cross of Christ*, 194. See also Morris, *Apostolic Preaching*, 157, 187-191, 206.

²⁵Irving M. Copi, *Introduction to Logic* (New York: Macmillan, 1972), 83.

²⁶John MacQuarrie, *God-Talk: An Examination of the Language and Logic of Theology* (New York: Harper and Row, 1967).

²⁷John McLeod Campbell, *The Nature of the Atonement and Its Relation to Remission of Sins and Eternal Life* (First published, 1856; reprint Beloved Publishing, 2015.)

²⁸P.T. Forsyth, *The Work of Christ* (London: Independent Press, 1958), 163.

²⁹Hastings Rashdall, *The Idea of the Atonement in Christian Theology: Being the Bampton Lectures for 1915* (London: Macmillan, 1919), 428, 454-455, probably borrowing from Abelard (c. 1079–1142).

³⁰Don S. Browning, *Atonement and Psychotherapy* (Philadelphia: Westminster, 1966).

³¹Gustaf Aulen, *Christus Victor* (New York: Macmillan, 1969); *The Faith of the Christian Church*. (London: SCM Press, 1960), 198ff, 204.

³²Anders Nygren, *Essence of Christianity: Two Essays* (Grand Rapids: Eerdmans, 1960).

³³Fisher Humphreys, *The Death of Christ* (Nashville: Broadman, 1978), whose work guided me to several of the cited authors on the atonement.

³⁴Stephen Finlan, *The Family Metaphor in Jesus' Teaching: Gospel Imagery and Application*, 2nd ed. (Eugene, OR: Cascade Books, 2013), 81-90. Finlan's entire book presents a fascinating exposition of the same theme as presented here. Unfortunately, I read Finlan's work only after I had essentially completed this manuscript. After I had completed this manuscript, Finlan published his latest book on this subject, *Salvation Not Purchased: Overcoming the Ransom Idea to Rediscover the Original Gospel Teaching* (Eugene, OR: Cascade Books, 2020).

Chapter 11
Tying Up Loose Ends

God loves us all and has pursued us all the way to the cross to bring us into the family of God.

Atonement Viewed through the Jesus Lens

The whole of Scripture from beginning to end narrates the drama of divine self-revelation. That drama also centered on atonement in that from Abraham to Moses to Jesus of Nazareth, God was reconciling humanity to himself. That continuing work of God constituted the heart of the revelation. The climax of that divine self-unveiling came in Jesus of Nazareth—preaching, teaching, dying, and rising again. Jesus proclaimed the good news that the kingdom of God has come in himself, the Father's Son. He called us to come home to fellowship with our loving Father and walk in faithfulness to him. The gospel according to Jesus centered on the Father—the Father's love, forgiveness, and family.

Although Jesus never used the word atonement or its equivalent, atonement viewed through the Jesus lens means reconciliation to our loving Father. Atonement does not require that someone—not even Jesus—placate God in order for him to forgive us. Atonement understood through the teaching of our Lord means our loving, gracious Father comes to us in his Son to reconcile us to himself simply by forgiving us. He does not require that anyone pay him anything to earn that forgiveness. He calls us only to repentance and faith and pursues us all the way to a Roman cross to effect that reconciliation. Atonement does not mean the appeasement of an angry God but reconciliation with our loving, gracious, forgiving Father.

Just the Beginning

The reconciliation with our heavenly Father that Jesus proclaimed, lived, and called humanity to experience encompasses far more than the atonement as traditionally conceived. Atonement as Jesus conceived it, although he never used the word or its equivalent, meant the entirety of our lives reconciled with God and transformed thereby. Most of Jesus' preaching had to do with how we live in this world in obedience to and in fellowship with our Father. This book has said little about these matters, but instead addresses how God reconciles us to himself—not what happens after we have come to experience fellowship with God. My purpose in this volume is to try to "get us off on the right foot." If we do not get the first step right, it's terribly hard to get the rest of the steps right. If we do not even understand what the first step is, how will we get the later steps right?

We have only touched on the concept of atonement in the New Testament as a whole following the Gospels; but my purpose was to try to understand our salvation as Jesus himself conceived it. I am willing for the moment to settle for a simple beginning: Jesus taught that our *Abba* loves us, invites us to come back home, and welcomes us with a barbeque cookout when we do. The gospel according to Jesus is all about the Father—nothing more, nothing less, nothing else.

Three Twenty-first-century Problems

Now it is time to acknowledge that some people have distinct problems with thinking about God as Father. These problems come in two different flavors.

A fellow seminarian once observed that he did not know how to imagine God. I replied naively that I had no such problem—I simply thought of God as my heavenly Father. "If you knew my old man," my friend replied, "you could never think of God as your father!"

I was taken aback. When he told me about his dad, however, I understood. I had experienced a very different kind of father. Mine was kind, loving, strong, supportive, and positive even when critical—an inspiring role model. On and on I could go singing the praises of my dad. I would never call him my "old man" either. I almost worshipped him. My friend had not experienced that kind of father; so, thinking of God as his Father, even his heavenly Father, felt too much like pulling God down to the level of his dad. Furthermore, it called up negative feelings about God himself.

More recently, women have raised other objections to calling God "Father." They have experienced men lording power over them either physically or economically, abusing them, violating them in various ways. For them to speak of God as Father is not merely sexist; it dredges up the darkest pictures of human maleness imaginable.

Even if they have not experienced men in malevolent ways, many women resent the idea that males are made in the image of God while females are not. They find offensive the idea that all the sin and evil in the world is the fault of women because Eve ate that first apple in the Garden of Eden. (Chapter 3, "The River That Waters the Earth," of my previous book *The Jesus Lens* refutes that nonsense.) For women of either mindset, presenting God as Father holds distinctly objectionable qualities.

I have a third kind of problem, however. My problem consists of my desire to be true to the divine self-disclosure in Jesus Christ on the one hand and finding my concept of God in conflict with certain elements of our culture on the other. How can I be faithful to the divine self-revelation in the history of Israel as witnessed to in

Scripture and climaxed in Jesus of Nazareth and still communicate that Good News to my twenty-first-century American peers?

Our culture is not that of first-century Palestine. We are twenty-first-century Americans, not first-century Jews. We live in an egalitarian democratic republic professing "freedom and justice for all," not in an explicitly male-dominated autocracy. We have not been immersed in the ideology of the Hebrew Scriptures but in the civic religion of American history and jurisprudence. Still, our Lord was a Jew, living in first-century Palestine, thinking and preaching like a first-century Palestinian Jew. How can we translate the gospel according to Jesus into a mode that communicates to a wide audience of informed, sophisticated twenty-first-century Americans?

A Possible Solution

I believe Jesus' conception of atonement in terms of his loving *Abba* can easily be translated into a manner of speaking that communicates to everyone. Although today we do not instinctively resonate with Israel's exodus from Egypt and return from exile or have a concept of the near-kin redeemer, we can understand those concepts from an ancient society. Even so, we do not feel the emotional power those associations held for ancient Hebrews.

At the same time, each of us needs family and yearns for love and acceptance. Even a man who grew up under a mean, vindictive father desires love, support, and affirmation. Even a woman who has experienced men in less than optimal ways desires personal relationship, love, and even admiration. Furthermore, we all need the security of knowing we have family who will rescue us in adversity.

The loving *Abba* concept of Jesus of Nazareth can easily be translated into a mode of thinking that meets the needs of each of the above imagined individuals as well as those comfortable with more traditional modes of thought. Just as John translated Jesus' kingdom of God into eternal life and Paul translated Christ's crucifixion into the forensic idea of justification, we can translate Jesus' concept of his *Abba* into pictures that communicate with our culture. A restatement of Jesus' idea of God and atonement might be this: God loves us all and has pursued us all the way to the cross to bring us into the family of God.

God loves you whether male or female, straight or gay or lesbian or transgender, black or white, American or Chinese, Christian or Muslim or Jew or Hindu, atheist or agnostic. Whoever you are, God loves you and desires a personal relationship with you. God so desires that relationship as to embody the totality of the divine nature in Jesus of Nazareth to reveal that self-sacrificing love, to embody that love in action, and to bestow God's love by pursuing the human race all the way to the cross.

Then why did Jesus have to die? Why couldn't God simply forgive us without the cross? Well, Jesus proclaimed that God did forgive us without the cross—before the cross. If Jesus had not come, however, how would we have recognized that forgiveness? In order to communicate his grace, bestow his forgiveness, and draw us to receive his fellowship, God embodied all he is in Jesus of Nazareth and pursued us all the way to the cross. The cross was not necessary for God's sake, but for ours. God did not need the cross to forgive us, but we needed the cross to recognize and receive God's grace, forgiveness, and fellowship.

The Effects of Atonement

To be fair to Anselm and Calvin, they were attempting to deal with the reality that humans have not only sinned against God, but in our ignorant and even deliberately evil intentions and deeds we have also deeply marred the image of God created into the human race. How do we deal with our guilt? How do we deal with the damage we have done to our psyches through our sin? How do we deal with the damage done to the human race, society, and culture by our ignorance and evil? Various theories of the atonement developed by Tertullian, Origen, Athanasius, Anselm, Calvin, and others we have mentioned attempted to answer these questions.

In contrast to the classical theories of the atonement, here is the way Jesus' unique message—one never conceived or proclaimed prior to him—answers those questions. First, our Father deals with our guilt simply by forgiving us. God counted Abraham's faith as righteousness (Rom. 4:3). God "justifies the ungodly," Paul said (v. 5). God does not demand satisfaction, expiation, propitiation, or repayment to set the accounts in order before he forgives. To do so would in reality constitute a refusal to forgive. Are we to believe that Jesus commanded us to do what God refuses to do—freely forgive without "satisfaction"? Are we to think that Jesus commanded us to be more merciful, gracious, forgiving, and righteous than God?

Forgiveness means God dismisses the debt and forgoes the punishment. God's free forgiveness—without reparations—does not mean God treats our sin lightly, as inconsequential. Instead, the very magnitude of human sin made the cross inevitable for Jesus of Nazareth. The Jewish authorities could not brook his implied claim to be the Son of God, at last clearly stated at his trial. The Roman authorities could not tolerate his claim to be Messiah, King of the Jews. Jesus' message, behavior, and implied claims, eventually plainly stated, made his crucified death inevitable in first-century Palestine. He did not draw back—even from crucifixion—in order to reveal God's self-sacrificial forgiveness in its fulness and to bestow God's grace on humanity. To that end, he voluntarily walked into Jerusalem to his death.[1]

Second, God deals with the damage we have done to ourselves by drawing us into the family of God, into fellowship with God. As we live in communion with our Creator and Redeemer, that intimate relationship transforms our character. God changes us "from glory to glory" (2 Cor. 3:18 KJV). God does not ignore our sin in forgiving us. God expiates our sin by forgiving our sin and guilt, drawing us into the family of God, and transforming our character by our communion with the divine Trinity.

Third, God sends us out into the world to transform our society and culture. Again, God does not ignore the damage humans have done to this beautiful creation. God forgives our sin and guilt, draws us into intimate fellowship, and then commissions us to go out as divine emissaries to rebuild this world one person at a time, one family at a time, one institution at a time in the power of the Holy Spirit. Even so, we still bear the imprint of the damage our ignorance and evil have done to our own psyches and to our societal structures.

Finally, God holds out to us the prospect that in the end we will go home to be gathered around the family hearth—"in my Father's house," Jesus said (John 14:2). We will be gathered around the family table in "the marriage supper of the lamb," as John wrote from Patmos (Rev. 19:9). "We will be like him [Christ], for we will see him as he is," one first-century pastor wrote to his flock (1 John 3:2). God will ultimately bring us fully into the image of God—the image of Christ—in eternity. That is consummated atonement—fulfilled reconciliation.

Jesus' Message and Its Context

Jesus preached that God our loving Father calls us to reconciliation with himself, without requiring that anyone pay satisfaction beforehand. That message stood on its own and did not rely on the cultural context of near-kin redemption for its truth. At the same time, the first-century church so heard that message as to state it repeatedly in terms recalling Israel's exodus from Egypt, their national redemption. This author sees God as Father as occurring within the cultural context of near-kin redemption; but Jesus' message did not rely on that connection for its validity.

Note

[1] I am indebted to my friend Tom Prevost for pointing out to me the marvelous passages in Paul Tillich's *Systematic Theology* that speak powerfully of the need to balance an emphasis on God as Father with God as Lord (I, 289-290), to balance divine forgiveness with divine wrath against sin (II, 77-78; not to be confused with wrath on the sinner). Tillich also provides a fine theological discussion of the nature of the Incarnation and its connection with atonement (II, 123-125, 173-180).

Conclusion

When Cultures Collide

When the gospel collides with culture, Christians have the choice of confronting and alienating, or corrupting through ignorance, or translating sympathetically; our culture, though, coincides in two respects with the culture of Jesus—as a narrative culture desiring love above all else.

Lords of the Earth[1]

Stan Dale plunged into the darkness of the Indonesian valley where the Yali of Irian Jaya lived. These cannibals thought the entire earth consisted of that valley overshadowed by the Snow Mountains. On that belief, they called themselves "lords of the earth." They found their greatest pleasure in shooting so many arrows into a man that the arrows stuck out of him "like the quills of a porcupine." Reserving their religious rites solely for the men, they cut their women off from all spiritual consolation. Consequently, the women committed suicide at an alarming rate, far surpassing that of the Yali men or of the women of neighboring tribes.

Stan was a Christian missionary, but he was also a man's man. He had no respect for preachers who minced words, who failed to tell the truth as it is. He waded into that primitive culture proclaiming that they were all sinners bound for hell unless they accepted Jesus Christ as Lord and Savior. Of course, those fierce warriors did not accept that message calmly. Stan engendered a great deal of hostility by his confrontational preaching. Eventually some of the Yalis believed in Jesus Christ and became Christians. His bold confrontational method worked. The fierce cannibal warriors' demeanor began to change in appearance from an "animal look" to a calm, peaceful yearning to hear the word of God.

One day Stan and his associate Phil Masters began walking deep into new Yali territory, areas they had never visited before. Alarmed at the arrival of the missionaries, the warriors of the area attacked them viciously. The evidence at the scene found by New Guinea officials a few days later told the story of their deaths, confirmed eventually by the Yali warriors who participated in the murders.

As the arrows pierced the bodies of the missionaries, they pulled them out, broke them, and dropped them on the ground. Terrified at this act of courage and strength, the Yalis shot their arrows even more desperately. When Stan and Phil at last succumbed to the hundreds of arrows, their bodies "as full of arrows as the quills of a porcupine," the warriors beheaded them and dismembered their bodies into small pieces. Only by such measures could they be sure the spirits of the white men would be truly dead. When the government officers found the scene days later, more than two hundred bloody broken arrows littered the gory beach where the missionaries had died.

Their manly courage so impressed those blood-thirsty warriors, however, that many of them converted to faith in Jesus Christ. Stan Dale and Phil Masters won to Jesus Christ as many Yalis in their deaths as they had won through their preaching.[2]

Peace Child[3]

Don Richardson entered a nearby territory of Papua New Guinea, an area claimed as home by the Sawi people. No white man had ever seen the Sawi territory on the Kronkel River when Richardson arrived. Painted warriors carrying spears met him, his wife Carol, and their four-month-old son Stephen on their arrival in the village of Kamur, escorted them to their home, and celebrated for three days.

The Richardsons witnessed fourteen hand-to-hand Sawi battles in their own front yard their first two months in their new home—warriors fighting over who got to have the missionaries live near them. The Sawis were headhunters and cannibals. To build up their own virility, they ate the flesh of enemies they had killed and slept on the skulls of those slain enemies.

Soon after arriving, Don began to go to the man-house where the men met to smoke and tell tall tales. In time, the warriors asked the missionary to tell them about his religion. As he narrated the story of Jesus, the men appeared bored, even sleepy. When he got to the story of Judas' betrayal of Jesus, though, they suddenly perked up. Richardson eventually realized with horror that they saw Judas as the hero of the story.

Then he learned that the Sawis held treachery as their highest cultural value. They especially honored betraying a friend—"fattening him with friendship for the slaughter"—like a pig. Over the ensuing months Don struggled to find a way to tell the story of the Good News of Jesus in a way that would resonate with these hardened Stone Age killers. Then he learned of the cultural practice of the "peace child." Two villages at war would swap infant children—hostages, if you will—to guarantee peace between them. Each "hostage" was known as a "peace child." Each village had the sacred responsibility of caring for and protecting the peace child given them by the other village.

Don also learned a story that still haunted Kamur. Hato had given his son as a peace child to the Kayagars—who killed and ate his son. Even with their celebration of "fattening with friendship for the slaughter," that sort of offense could not be allowed to stand.

The missionary then returned to the man-house and told Jesus' story framed in a new format. This time he said that God, to make peace with humanity, had given his Son, Jesus, as the Peace Child. Judas betrayed him; and humanity killed him. With that story the gospel broke through. The village of Kamur, along with other surrounding villages, accepted God's Peace Child, Jesus, as Lord and Savior.

Sometime later, the Richardsons hosted a great feast in the front yard of their home. As the dugout canoes arrived from village after village, a commotion erupted on the river bank. The missionary went down to the landing spot to investigate and saw a man lying deathly ill and helpless in the bottom of a dugout. As Don knelt examining the man, he heard a voice behind him.

"You won't give medicine to that man, will you?"

It was the voice of Amio, son of Hato, whose child had been eaten by the Kayagars.

Taking him by the earlobes in the Sawi manner of chastisement, Don said, "Amio, I plead the Peace Child."

"The peace child my father gave is dead!" the Sawi warrior cried out in anguish, remembering his brother. "This man killed him."

"But the Peace Child God gave still lives," Richardson replied. "And because he lives, you may not take vengeance. Forgive this man, Amio, for Jesus' sake."

Trembling, Amio picked up the helpless warrior from the canoe and carried him in his arms up to Don's house for treatment.[4]

Confronting, Translating, or Corrupting

These contrasting stories show two of the choices Christians face when our Good News collides with an alien culture. Stan Dale held in contempt any effort to translate the message he had received from his tradition into the culture to which he preached. The Yalis killed him and his associate. Ultimately, Stan and Christ won, but at what a price.

Don Richardson, on the other hand, took time truly to understand the Sawi culture. He found the entry point into the mind of those warriors and translated the gospel into language they could understand. Stan confronted the Yalis with the harsh version of the gospel he had received from his tradition, and died for it. Don translated the gospel into the Sawi cultural language, and led that tribe into fellowship with their heavenly Father without destroying himself and his family.

That dynamic has played out from the beginning of the Christian faith. The Synoptic Gospels (Mark followed by Matthew and Luke) told the story of Jesus in the Hebraic cultural model in which Jesus preached. John, by contrast, wrote his gospel translated into a new idiom designed to speak to a Greek culture. He opened his gospel with a marvelous meditation on the Word (the *Logos*)—echoing

Wisdom of the Book of Proverbs on the Hebrew side and Zeno's *logos* on the Greek philosophical side.

The Synoptics emphasized the kingdom of God of the loving Father, but John translated the kingdom into eternal life granted by the loving Father. He emphasized the Father, however, three times as often as he mentioned eternal life. He so successfully translated the gospel to communicate to an alien culture that two thousand years later his gospel still remains the favorite of many believers. If we think of God as our loving Father who gives us eternal life, we probably owe that conception to the Fourth Gospel.

When the apostles of Jesus went out to preach the gospel, they no doubt preached it much the way Jesus did—a Hebraic story for their Hebrew people. Then when Saul of Tarsus converted, this Jew conversant with Greek culture captured a new vision. Why not preach the gospel in a way that would communicate with Gentiles who knew nothing of Temple ritual and sacrifice, Exodus and Exile, Hebrew near-kin redeemers, and such?

Accordingly, Paul found other metaphors for the gospel of Jesus Christ. He kept Jesus' metaphor of the loving *Abba*, which he used frequently; but he also translated Jesus' gospel into other graphic pictorial scenes. In Galatians and Romans, he used the courtroom metaphor of justification. In Colossians 1:13 he briefly stated the gospel in terms of Jesus the conquering warrior leading us from the kingdom of darkness into the kingdom of light. On and on he went, through metaphor after metaphor, picture after picture, never tiring of finding new ways to state that beautiful story. He determined to find a way to appeal to each of his listeners. "All things to all people, that I might by all means save some," he said (1 Cor. 9:20). Consequently, even today many of us learned the gospel the way Paul preached and wrote it.

A thousand years after Paul, Archbishop Anselm translated the gospel into the language of his culture. Anselm told the story of Jesus in the language of Norman feudalism, with God's honor violated and satisfaction demanded. He found a translation that truly communicated with his culture. No doubt, as soon as his translation was out there, priests all over Europe and the British Isles began to tell the story that way. Almost certainly, additionally, Anselm's "gospel" communicated and attracted many to faith in Jesus.

Anselm, however, made a critical error in his translation. He made that error innocently, but he made it all the same. His culture, that of the medival priests in Norman Frankish kingdoms, did not understand the cultural context or language in which Jesus had lived and preached. Their ignorance did not come deliberately; it went all the way back to the Greek fathers of the church from the second century onward. Consequently, without intending to do so, Anselm corrupted the gospel. He did not truly translate it; he corrupted it into a story vastly different from the one Jesus told and lived. Then through that same sort of ignorance, John Calvin in Geneva followed Anselm's error. True, Calvin reworded Anselm's version slightly, but not enough to matter. Calvin's version stood no closer to Jesus of Nazareth than did Anselm's.

Now today, 900 years after Anselm and 500 years after Calvin, a horde of twenty-first-century people reject the gospel of Jesus Christ because they have only heard it told in Anselm's and Calvin's corruptions of it—a story that no longer speaks to many in our culture. They have never heard the pure gospel of God who loves us so much that he pursues us all the way to the cross. They think they reject the gospel of Jesus Christ and the New Testament, but they do not. They reject the way it has been preached; and their rejection of Jesus is our fault, not theirs. Somehow, too many in the church have lost sight of the marvelous Good News that God loves the wayward children and holds nothing back in the effort to bring us home and transform us as individuals and societies through communion with God through the Holy Spirit.

When Cultures Coincide

When the gospel collides with our contemporary culture, Christians have the choice of confronting and alienating, corrupting through ignorance, or translating sympathetically. We are blessed, however, to stand at a point in history when our culture actually coincides with that original Hebraic culture of Jesus in at least two significant ways.

First, our culture, like that of Jesus, is a narrative culture—at least the post-modern generation is. (I make this observation without intending to assert any evaluation whatever on post-modernism.) In the words of a song from the South Georgia musical *Swamp Gravy*, "I have a story, you have a story, we all have a story to tell."[5] We can present the gospel as a story—the narrative of the supremely loving and gracious Father (or Parent, for those whose experiences make them cringe at "Father"). We do not have to explain it in the abstract philosophical language of the academy. We do not have to preach it like superior beings telling lesser mortals The Truth from on high. People respond far more readily to a story than to a sermon.

Secondly, our culture desires love above all else. We desire love even above success. We may not always act like it, but we do. Many people have never known the love of a strong and faithful father, or an intelligent and wise mother, or of a supportive husband, or of an encouraging wife, or even of a faithful friend. Our society finds itself so starved for love that we will grab its counterfeit any place one shows up. That craving partially explains the rise of deadly cults and the popularity of political conspiracy theories. Acceptance from any group will substitute if genuine family goes missing.

Jesus' familial metaphor of the loving Father that resonated in a culture familiar with the idea of God as the near-kin Redeemer may not always resonate with many of our neighbors. We are blessed, though, in that we do not have to limit ourselves to a single metaphor but can move on into Jesus' actual message of redemption—the surpassing love of God. The author of First John moved beyond Jesus' metaphor of the Father to state the gospel in its purest, most literal sense—God is love (1 John 4:8). To be sure, this statement is still something of a metaphor, for it depends in part on our experience of love from other humans. Still, it stands so close to literal truth that the metaphor ceases to be just another metaphor. As Paul put it, "God was in Christ, reconciling the world to himself" (2 Cor. 5:19 KJV).

The story of the loving God of heaven who so loves us as to embody the divine nature and character in a village carpenter to communicate that love, to give that love, to hold nothing back, not even turning back from a Roman torture stake, bestowing that love through a lonely agonizing death—that story communicates.

People instinctively realize it must be true. Jesus must have lived. If he had not, who would have made him up? Greeks celebrating either red hot Dionysian revels or ice-cold Athenian rationality could not. Romans glorifying the blood-stained warrior and the obscenely wealthy senator or Caesar would not. Jews showed themselves unlikely candidates to create such a fiction by their reaction to Jesus when he did appear. No one before Jesus had envisioned such a God, as far as we know. If Jesus had not lived, if Jesus had not embodied God's nature and character, then who would have been the genius to invent him?

We only have to learn to tell that story as effectively as Jesus did. In order to do that, however, we have to stand ready to live without political power, as he did. We cannot preach the gospel of Jesus Christ while grasping after wealth and political and military might and persecuting our enemies. Even more, we have to be ready to die as he did. That is why he said, "Take up your cross and follow me" (Matt. 16:24).

When people come to know this God of infinite forgiveness, grace, and love, and learn to commune with the Holy Spirit on a daily basis, they will find their own psyches transformed one day at a time. When enough people learn to live in that divine grace, sacrificing themselves for others as Jesus did, entire societies will be transformed—one life, one family, and one social institution at a time. The gospel according to Jesus has no shortfall in it, no inability to communicate and transform. Jesus' gospel simply has not been proclaimed consistently. Our generation has not rejected Jesus' gospel. The truth is, many people of our generation have yet to *hear* the gospel according to Jesus.

Notes

[1] This story is told in Don Richardson, *Lords of the Earth* (Ventura, CA: Regal, 1977).
[2] Ibid., 170, 287, 307-308, 314.
[3] This story is told in Don Richardson, *Peace Child* (Glendale, CA: Regal, 1974).
[4] Ibid., 34, 215, 268.
[5] *Swamp Gravy: Georgia's Official Folk-Life Play* (Colquitt/Miller Arts Council, Colquitt, GA)

Appendices

Redemption Vocabulary in the Old Testament

Ancient Hebrews had four major word-groups to express the concept of *redemption*—three in Hebrew and one in Greek. Let's take them one at a time, attempting to see how Jews prior to the first century used these words and how the Scriptures read by Jesus' contemporaries used them.

Kaphar/Kopher (Atone/Atonement)

The first Hebrew word-group we will consider consisted of *kaphar* (atone), *kopher*, and *kippurim* (atonement). These words usually occur in a religious setting (dedication of priests—Exod. 29:36-37; the Day of Atonement—Lev. 23:27-28, 25:9; Num. 29:11). Occasionally these words appear in a ritual setting meaning to purchase the life of the individual at a price (related to a census—Exod. 30:10-16; denied to a murderer—Num. 35:31, 32). This word-group also appears in non-ritual or secular contexts to mean to buy off an adversary for an offense against him (Exod. 21:30; Num. 5:8; Prov. 6:35; 13:8). This usage is regularly translated into English as "ransom," even though it never means to ransom an individual kidnapped or captured and held for ransom as we almost always use that word.

Padah (Liberate at a Price)

The second word-group translated "redeem" consisted of various forms of the Hebrew word *padah*, meaning to liberate by purchase—"for a price."⁶ Because of its implication of a price paid, this word and its derivatives are frequently translated "ransom." Even so, it never carries in Scripture our concept of a person kidnapped and held for ransom. Still, it always means to set free for a price, whether from slavery, debt, or obligation to God. This word often appears in sacral situations in which a person pays the price for his life to the Temple, parallel to or sometimes synonymously with such use of the *kaphar* group mentioned above. *Padah* often referred metaphorically to God's redemption of Israel in the Exodus parallel to the *ga'al* group discussed in the following section. In that usage, it meant to liberate, to rescue. Chapter 2 develops that use of redemption language as communicated through the *padah* word group.

Old Testament Redemption Vocabulary

HEBREW (transliterated)	MEANING	SEPTUAGINT (Sample texts)
ga'al[1]	To redeem as near kin	λυτροω (lutroo)[2] Exod. 6:6, 15:13; Lev. 25:25, 48; Ps. 69:18; Isa. 43:1; Jer. 31:11
ge'ulah	Near-kin redemption	λυτρωσις (lutrosis): Lev. 25:29, 48 λυτρα (lutra, pl. of lutron) Lev. 25:24, 26
go'el	Near-kin redeemer	λυτρομενος (lutromenos) Prov. 23:11, Isa. 41:14, Jer. 27:34 ‘ρυσαμενος (‘rusamenos) Isa. 44:6; 47:4; 48:17; 49:7, 26 ‘ρυσαι (‘rusai) Isa. 63.16 [continued on next page]
		’εξαιρουμενος (‘exairoumenos) Isa. 60:16 ’αγχιστευων (‘agchisteuon; next of kin) Ruth 3:9, 12; 4:4, 6, 8, 14 λυτροτης (lutrotes) Ps. 19:14, 78:35 (only uses)
padah	To purchase at a price	λυτροω[3] (lutroo) Lev. 27:29, Num. 18:15 λυτρωσις (lutrosis) Num. 18:16 ‘ρυσομαι (‘rusomai; deliver) Hos. 13:14
peduyim[1] peduth	A purchase for a price, a bribe or pay-off	λυτρωσις (lutrosis) Ps. 111:9, 129:7 λυτρα (lutra, pl. of lutron) Exod. 21:30
kopher	Atonement[4]	λυτρον[5] (lutron): only in Prov. 6:35, 13:8 λυτρα (lutra, pl. of lutron) Exod. 21:30, 30:12

Ga'al/Go'el (Near-kin Redemption/Redeemer)

The third Hebrew word-group meaning "redeem"—*ga'al*—carried the implicit meaning of the nearest kin acting as redeemer (the *go'el*, rescuer, liberator) for a relative in trouble.[7] This concept found legislative definition in Leviticus 25:25-55. Whenever we read "next of kin," or "redeem," or "kinsman-redeemer" in the New Revised Standard Version or the New International Version of Ruth 3 and 4, for example, some form of this word-group lies in the Hebrew background. *Ga'al* often referred metaphorically to God's redemption of Israel in the Exodus and in their return from Exile. In that usage, authors represented Yahweh as Israel's near-kin "Redeemer." Chapters 3 and 4 develop this concept as communicated through the *ga'al* word group.

While both *padah* and *ga'al* meant "to redeem," there did exist a difference of connotation. *Ga'al* emphasized that the redeemer was the next of kin, while *padah* indicated that the redemption was "for a price." The near-kin redeemer, however, usually paid the "price" for the redemption, even when the writer used *padah*,[8] except when the price had to do with Temple ritualistic redemption. *Padah* and *ga'al* overlapped in the idea of liberation. Additional overlap of meaning came about through their use synonymously with one another, so that *padah* frequently acquired some of the connotations of *ga'al* as near-kin redemption. These two Hebrew words occur as synonyms in Leviticus 25:25-55, 27:27-29; Jeremiah 31:11; Hosea 13:14; and Psalms 69:18, where *padah* seems to acquire the connotation of near-kin redemption.

Λυτροω (*lutroo*, Redeem)

The fourth word-group—in Greek, this time—appears in a book most Christians have never heard of. In the third-second centuries BCE, Hebrew scholars in Alexandria, Egypt, translated the Hebrew Scriptures into Greek. Legends said 70 scholars each translated the Scriptures identically—word-for-word—in 70 days. For that reason, this Greek translation of the Hebrew Scriptures came to be known as the Septuagint (from the Latin word *septuaginta*, meaning "seventy"). Scholars abbreviate it LXX.

In the Septuagint, the Greek word-group based on λυτροω (*lutroo*, LU-TRAH-OH, meaning "redeem") translates *ga'al* 45 times; 42 times it translates *padah*.[9] This balance shows that in the Hebrew mind both *ga'al* and *padah* meant approximately the same thing—"to redeem, to liberate." Because of usage in the Septuagint, this Greek word-group took on the meanings of both Hebrew words they rendered. Thus, the Greek word-group based on λυτροω came to mean both to liberate (from *padah*), and near-kin redemption/redeemer (from *ga'al/go'el*). Since, however, *ga'al* and *padah* sometimes appeared as synonyms, the connotation of near-kin redemption came to overshadow this Greek word, even when used to translate *padah*.

Abba, *Father*

In a very few cases, a noun from the λυτροω group translated *kopher* (atonement). (See "Old Testament Redemption Vocabulary," p. 116.) The plural λυτρα (*lutra*)—but never the singular λυτρον (*lutron*)—rendered *kaphar/kopher* when that Hebrew word-group referred to the Temple tax paid for a life in a census. The singular noun never appears in the LXX in the religious sense of atonement or redemption; the plural noun was never used to refer to atonement for sin. The singular λυτρον (*lutron*) appears only twice in the Old Testament and then only in a non-ritual, secular sense (Prov. 6:35, 13:8).[10]

Notes

[1] *Ga'al* and *peduyim* are synonymous in Lev. 25:26-52, 27:27-29; Jer. 31:11; Hos. 13:14; and Ps. 69:18.

[2] Examples only, not exhaustive; λυτροω translates *ga'al* 45 times in LXX (Gerhard Kittel, *Theological Dictionary of the New Testament*, trans. and ed. Geoffrey W. Bromiley [Grand Rapids: Eerdmans, 1967], IV, 332).

[3] Examples only, not exhaustive; λυτροω translates *padah* 42 times in LXX (Ibid.).

[4] *Kopher* ordinarily meaning "atonement," usually translated by 'ιλασκω or 'εξιλασκω and derivatives.

[5] λυτρον/λυτρα rarely used in LXX to translate *kopher* (atonement); only when meaning "ransom."

[6] See R. Laird Harris, et al, eds. *Theological Wordbook of the Old Testament* (Chicago: Moody, 1980), I, 716-717.

[7] See Ibid., 144-145; and G. Johannes Botterweck and Helmer Ringgren, eds., *Theological Dictionary of the Old Testament* (Grand Rapids: Eerdmans, 1975), II, 350-355.

[8] Harris, *Theological Wordbook*, II, 716; Botterwick, *Theological Dictionary*, II, 351.

[9] Ibid.

[10] Additional material on redemption vocabulary found in the Hebrew Old Testament and the Greek Septuagint appears in "Old Testament Redemption Vocabulary." The reader desiring still further discussion of these Hebrew and Greek words can find it in the following works: Harris et. al., *Theological Wordbook of the Old Testament*, I, #300 *ga'al*, 144-145 and II, #1734 *pada*, 716-717; Botterweck and Ringgren, *Theological Dictionary of the Old Testament*, II, 350-355; and O. Proksch, *Theological Dictionary of the New Testament* (Grand Rapids: Eerdmans, 1967), IV, 328-335.

Redemption Vocabulary in the New Testament

Redemption vocabulary related to λυτρον/*lutron* or λυτροω/*lutroo* occurs twenty times in the New Testament. Since the Septuagint of the Old Testament regularly used the same Greek word both for "liberation at a price" and for "near-kin redemption," the obvious question arises: "Then what precisely do the New Testament occurrences of this word-group mean?" Before delving into that question, we need to take a look at another group of words also translated "redeem" in the writings of Paul and the Book of Revelation.

Market Place Terminology

The first two words we examine are 'αγοραζω (*agorazo*) and 'εξαγοραζω (*exagorazo*), both built on 'αγορα (*agora*), the market place. The verb 'αγοραζω means to purchase in the market place. Most of the New Testament uses of 'αγοραζω refer to literal market transactions (Matt. 13:44, 21:12; Mark 11:15; Luke 9:13; John 4:8; 1 Cor. 7:30; Rev. 18:11). (See "New Testament Redemption Vocabulary," p. 120.) Several times 'αγοραζω carries the metaphorical meaning of our having been purchased—redeemed—by Jesus Christ. The expressions "bought with a price" (1 Cor. 6:20, 7:23) and "with your blood you purchased" (Rev. 5:9 NIV; cf. 14:3, 4) indicate the extremely costly nature of our redemption by Jesus Christ—at the cost of his own life. In this usage, the translation "ransom" seems a highly inexact, even incorrect, rendering, even if frequently employed.

A similar word, 'εξαγοραζω, means an "'intensive buying,' i.e., a buying which exhausts the possibilities available."[1] This word occurs only in the Pauline literature four times and always in a metaphorical sense. Twice this word appears as "buying up the time" (Eph. 5:16, Col. 4:5). The other two instances of 'εξαγοραζω occur in Galatians 3:13 and 4:5, where Paul refers to our redemption by Christ Jesus metaphorically as a market-place purchase in which we have been "totally bought out" from the curse of the law. He then goes on to say in 5:1, "For freedom Christ has set us free. Stand firm, therefore, and do not submit again to a yoke of slavery," echoing 3:13 and consistently with 4:5. These statements suggest that Paul's emphasis here is on liberation.

Liberation Terminology

For the Old Testament background of these words, see "Redemption Vocabulary in the Old Testament" and "Old Testament Redemption Vocabulary." The Septuagint's use of these words in the Old Testament is fairly uncontroversial. When we get to the New Testament, however, the precise meaning and connotations of the redemption vocabulary built around λυτροω ceases to be simple.

New Testament Redemption Vocabulary

GREEK	MEANING	TEXTS
λυτροω (*lutroo*)	Redeem, liberate	Luke 1:68, 2:38, 24:21; Titus. 2:14; 1 Pet. 1:18
Λυτρον (*lutron*) ’Αντιλυτρon (*antilutron*)	Manumission, emancipation	Mark 10:45 = Matt 20:28 > 1 Tim 2:6
λυτρωτης (*lutrotes*)	Liberator	Acts 7:35. [only appearance in NT—of Moses, Israel's "liberator"—usual words for God as "Redeemer" in LXX were λυτρομενος (*lutromenos*) or ‘ρυσαμενος (‘*rusamenos*]
λυτρωσις (*lutrosis*)	Redemption	Heb. 9:12
’απολυτρωσις (*apolutrosis*)	Redemption	Luke 21:28; Rom. 3:24, 8:23; 1 Cor. 1:30; Eph. 1:7, 14; 4:30; Col. 1:14; Heb. 9:15, 11:35
’αγοραζω (*agorazo*)	Buy in the market, redeem	Literal: Matt. 13:44; 14:15; 21:12; 25:9, 10; Mark 6:36, 37; 11:15; 15:46; Luke 9:13, 22:36; John 4:8, 6:5, 13:29; 1 Cor. 7:30; Rev. 13:17, 18:11 Metaphorical: 1 Cor. 6:20, 7:23; 2 Pet. 2:1; Rev. 3:18; 5:9; 14:3, 4
’εξαγοραζω (*exagorazo*)	Buy up completely, redeem	Gal. 3:13, 4:5; Eph. 5:16; Col. 4:5

Derivation

F. Buchsel tells us that the word-group derives originally from λυω (*luo*; to loose).[2] The suffix -τρον (indicating a "means") was added to the verb root λυ-, creating the word λυτρον—the price by which a person is set free. Then from this noun arose the verb λυτροω—to redeem, to liberate.

Again, however, λυτρον never, meant "ransom" as we use the word—a person kidnapped or captured and held for ransom. It did regularly mean the manumission or emancipation price for a slave. Even though scholars regularly translate *lutron* as "ransom," it should actually be translated as manumission, emancipation, or liberation.

Septuagint Usage

The situation gets complicated by the Septuagint's use of the λυτροω group to translate both *padah* (liberate) and *ga'al* (liberate as a near kinsman). This Greek word-group thus sometimes meant simply liberate and other times meant near-kin redemption in the Septuagint. Furthermore, the Septuagint used this word-group to translate *kaphar* and *kopher* in both the religious sense of "atonement" and the religious sense of purchase or the secular sense of "buy off" or "bribe."

In light of this history, we have to answer the following questions: Which Septuagint usage(s) resonated in the first-century church? Did the Greek λυτροω words mean "near-kin redemption" for Jesus' contemporaries and the first-century church as they often did for the translators of the Septuagint when translating *ga'al*? Or did they mean *liberate* at a price or simply "liberation" as they sometimes did when translating *padah* or even *kaphar*? Or did all three Septuagint backgrounds prevail in different contexts?

Contemporary Debate

Procksch argues that these words mean simply liberation.[3] Leon Morris, on the other hand, argues that the meaning of this word-group meant "ransom" in the strict sense of "a price paid."[4] Morris, though, holds to a variety of the penal substitution theory of the atonement and can be suspected of arguing his theology at this point. Morris is joined in his opinion by John Murray, F.W. Grosheide, Richard E. Melick, and J. Ramsey Michaels, among a host of other scholars. Many other equally eminent scholars disagree, however. Among these latter interpreters are B.F. Westcott, as cited in Sandy and Headlam (*Romans*, ICC, 86), C.H. Dodd, N.T. Wright, James D.G. Dunn, and Andrew T. Lincoln.

Dunn, for instance, comments that the stronger the LXX influence is seen to be, the less it is likely a person will jump to the conclusion that this word-group means exclusively "paying a price."[5] That is to say, to adopt the ransom at a price view of these words flows from failure to consider the evidence from the Septuagint. Similarly, Lincoln comments, "[I]t appears to be over-dogmatic to insist on ransom connotations."[6] In other words, Lincoln thinks the exclusively "ransom at a price" interpretation results from a prior theological commitment.

After the publication of the Greek Septuagint, it would seem that for Jews, those words would no longer have meant only to emancipate or to liberate. The Septuagint translators had used them frequently to translate words in the *ga'al* Hebrew word-group, referring to near-kin redemption, even more often than to render the *padah* group, meaning *ransom*. For this reason, it seems obvious that the Greek words used to translate the *ga'al* vocabulary would often have taken on much of the meaning, at least connotatively, of that Hebrew word-group. Arguments exist on all sides of the debate; but the following factors guide my thinking:

- We should begin determining the meaning of this word-group for first-century Jewish Christians by examining the Septuagint rather than secular or other non-biblical sources. After all, the Septuagint constituted the secondary Scriptures for both first-century Jews and the early church and thereby molded their understanding of Greek vocabulary.

- The major importance of this word-group in the Septuagint is that of near-kin redemption, frequently translating the Hebrew *ga'al* group with its emphasis on the *go'el*, the near-kin redeemer. Even the Hebrew *padah* group by parallelism and synonymous usage often acquires the *ga'al* meaning of near-kin redemption. In this usage, the Hebrew and Greek words frequently described Israel's redemption from slavery in the Exodus and from exile in the Return. When λυτροω translates one of the latter group of verses, it frequently still means near-kin redemption connotatively, even though the *padah* Hebrew group does not focus on the *go'el*. Synonymous usage of the two Hebrew words in numerous texts produces that connotation. (See "Old Testament Redemption Vocabulary," p. 116.)

- When examined closely, differences in detail between the forms favored in the New Testament as compared to the Septuagint (Morris' argument in defense of his "ransom at a price" view) sometimes appear to represent no more than the stylistic preferences of Hellenistic Jews. Mark's word λυτρον, for instance, becomes ἀντιλυτρον in 1 Timothy, but with the same meaning as λυτρον in Mark. We even see the same New Testament author using two different forms in the same passage. For example, Hebrews 9:12 uses λυτρωσις, but three verses later 9:15 uses ἀπολυτρωσις. A compound form of this word-group, therefore, does not necessarily alter its meaning, often being merely stylistic, but not always.

- Finally, we should examine each use of a word in its literary context in determining its precise meaning in that passage. When we examine the New Testament use of the λυτροω/ἀπολυτροω word-groups in context, we find three different uses of these words.

Contextual Considerations

When we examine the New Testament use of the λυτροο / ἀπολυτροω word-groups in context, we find three different uses of these words.

Near-kin Redemption

Various forms of this word group appear 20 times in the New Testament. In five passages, the λυτροω and ἀπολυτροω vocabulary seems to refer clearly and explicitly to near-kin redemption:

- Luke 1:68 reads, "[H]e has looked favorably on his people and redeemed them."
- Romans 8:15-25 combines God as *Abba*, the family of God, and redemption in such a way as to show that Paul saw the intricate connection of those ideas.
- Ephesians 1:2,7, 14 speak of our "redemption as God's own people," tying that redemption to "God our Father."
- Colossians 1:2, 13-14 speak of our having been "rescued from the power of darkness and transferred . . . into the kingdom of his beloved Son," again tying that rescue to "God our Father." This statement clearly refers to Israel's redemption in the Exodus and entry into Canaan.
- Titus 2:2, 14 says Jesus "gave himself for us that he might redeem us . . . a people of his own," once more after having described God as "the Father."
- In 1 Peter 1:3-21, having described God twice as "Father," Peter tells us we were "redeemed" with "the precious blood of Christ, a lamb without blemish or defect." Here the author ties redemption to the Fatherhood of God and implies a parallel to Israel's redemption in the Exodus.

In no less than six New Testament passages by three to six different authors (depending on how we attribute the authorship of the books), the authors connect the redemption metaphor to a family metaphor in which God is Father and to Israel's Exodus from Egypt. Clearly the connection of God as Father with redemption, parallel to the Exodus, resonated widely in the first-century church. Furthermore, in the next section we will see that at least the connotation of near-kin redemption appears to occur in ten other uses of this word when used to recall Israel's liberation in their Exodus from Egypt.

Exodus as Liberation

Examined in their New Testament context, the λυτροο and 'απολυτροω vocabulary most often meant liberation at the very least (Acts 7:35; Rom. 3:24, 8:23; Eph. 4:30; Heb. 11:35; 1 Pet. 1:18). Luke probably used these words in the sense of liberation, recalling Israel's Exodus from Egypt (Luke 1:68, 2:38, 21:38, 24:21) when taken in the light of Luke 9:31. The context of each of these uses either supports or is consistent with this meaning and historical reference to Israel's Exodus from slavery in Egypt. Since the Old Testament proclaimed God as Israel's near-kin Redeemer in the Exodus and return from Exile, that idea probably adhered connotatively to these uses of the same vocabulary, even when it meant "liberation."

We observed earlier that in Galatians 3:13 and 4:5, Paul used the word 'εξαγοραζω (translated in our English Bibles as "redeem") and then stated that Christ has set us free (Gal. 5:1). In a somewhat parallel passage, Paul later used the word ἀπολυτρωσιν with reference to our bodies shortly after having stated that the entire creation will be "liberated from its bondage to decay" (Rom. 8:21, 23). For Paul, both words clearly meant at the very least to liberate, to set free.

Sacrifice of Atonement

In one passage the λυτροω and ἀπολυτροω vocabulary appears to refer connotatively to a sacrifice of atonement (Heb. 9:12, 15). Possibly this use developed out of the Septuagint practice of using the plural λυτρα (*lutra*) to translate the *kaphar* Hebrew group when referring to purchasing a life ritually in a census or for a personal capital offense. Hebrews 9:12 probably refers to the sacrifices on the Day of Atonement.

Thus, this word-group appears to have embodied a rich set of denotations and connotations flowing from Israel's history and uses in translating its Hebrew Scriptures into Greek. All these meanings and associations could often have imposed themselves on the Jewish mind simultaneously. In every New Testament occurrence of this word group except two, these words are consistent with a reference to Israel's redemption in the Exodus and return from Exile, with the connotation of God as the near-kin Redeemer.

Conclusions

Considering the Septuagint usage of this vocabulary group along with the context of these words in the New Testament indicates this group of words in the first century could be used with all three meanings found in the Septuagint. These words usually meant liberation, drawing an implicit parallel with Israel's Exodus from Egypt and return from the Babylonian Exile. With this reference to Israel's history, near-kin redemption probably always lurked in the background of the thinking of first century Jews. Often, these words at least connoted or even denoted near-kin redemption. Finally, this word-group was once (but only once) used in the sense of atonement, harking back to Israel's sacrificial system whereby a man's life was purchased in a census or when guilty of some capital offence against another. To complicate matters still further, frequently the same word is susceptible of more than one meaning simultaneously due to contextual implications.

I conclude, therefore, that the λυτροω and ἀπολυτροω words in the New Testament usually denote at least "liberation" but often also mean "near-kin redemption," at least connotatively. Finally, in Mark 10:45/Matthew 20:28 the word λυτρον means "manumission" or "emancipation" (not "ransom" as we almost universally use that word), with no hint of a price being paid to anyone. This word would call to mind for a first-century Jew Israel's liberation from slavery in the Exodus and from exile in the Return, with the implication of God as Israel's near-kin Redeemer.

Notes

[1] F. Buchsel, *Theological Dictionary of the New Testament*, Gerhard Kittel, gen. ed. (Grand Rapids: Eerdmans, 1967), I, 128.

[2] Ibid., IV, 340.

[3] Ibid., IV.

[4] Leon Morris, *The Apostolic Preaching of the Cross* (Grand Rapids: Eerdmans, 1956), 11–59.

[5] James D.G. Dunn, *Word Biblical Commentary: Romans 1–8* (Dallas: Word, 1988), 169.

[6] Andrew T. Lincoln, *Word Biblical Commentary: Ephesians* (Dallas: Word, 1990), 28.

Glossary

Apocrypha—religious books the Jews held in high regard but did not consider Scripture, in the Catholic Bible and originally in the King James Version of the Bible.

Aramaic—the ancient language of the Aramaeans that had come to serve as the international language by the first century and was the local native language of Jesus.

Atonement—a word that literally means at-one-ment. The classical theories of the Atonement attempted to explain in legal terms how Jesus saves us from our sins. This work presents atonement in terms of personal and familial relationship, as God as our heavenly Father reconciling us to himself.

Expiation—the removal of sin by some act on our behalf.

Josephus—a first-century (37–100 CE) Jewish general and historian who wrote several books that inform us greatly concerning the ancient history of Israel.

Justification—a courtroom legal term that is roughly equivalent to our word "acquit" but meaning to declare righteous, in the right. In Paul's usage, it meant "to declare right with God."

Penal Substitution Theory of the Atonement—the theory of John Calvin (1509–1564) of Geneva, Switzerland. Jesus suffered punishment we earned by offending God's justice.

Propitiation—the means by which someone who is angry or hostile to someone else is rendered friendly. Synonyms are appeasement and placation.

Satisfaction—compensation for loss sustained. In feudalism, satisfaction restored what a feudal lord had lost to his honor through "treason" by a vassal.

Satisfaction Theory of the Atonement—the theory advanced by Archbishop Anselm of Canterbury in 1097 in his book *Cur Deus Homo*. Anselm saw Jesus as paying the compensation we owe to God for having offended his honor and justice.

Septuagint (LXX)—the ancient Greek translation of the Hebrew Scripture produced by Jewish scholars in Alexandria, Egypt in the third century.

Son of Man—In Daniel 7:14, the representative of Israel who receives glory and power. Jesus adopted this expression to refer to himself on a regular basis.

Suffering Servant—In Isaiah 40–55, the people of Israel who are called to be a "light to the nations." In Isaiah 53, someone who suffers and dies on behalf of Israel. Jesus alluded to Isaiah's Suffering Servant passages several times and clearly thought of himself as the fulfillment of Isaiah's Suffering Servant.

Bibliography

History

Brooke, Christopher. *From Alfred to Henry III: 871–1271*. New York: Norton, 1971.

Devi-McGleish, Yasmin and J. David Cox. "From Weregild to a Way Forward? English Restorative Justice in Its Historical Context." https://www.wlv.ac.uk/media/departments/faculty-of-social-sciences/documents/wolverhampton-law-journal/5.-Devi-McGleish-and-Cox.pdf.

Durant, Will. *Story of Civilization: The Age of Faith*. Vol. 4, *The Story of Civilization*. New York: Simon and Schuster, 1950.

Gies, Joseph and Frances. *Life in a Medieval Castle*. New York: Perennial, 1974.

Hamilton, Sarah. *The Practice of Penance, 900–1050*. London: Boydell, 2001.

Hollister, C. Warren. *Henry I*. New Haven, CT: Yale, 2001.

Howarth, David. *1066: The Year of the Conquest*. Dorset Press, 1977.

Johnson, Paul. *A History of Christianity*. New York: Atheneum, 1977.

Lea, Henry Charles. *History of Auricular Confession and Indulgences in the Latin Church*. 3 vols. New York: Greenwood, 1896.

MacCulloch, Diarmaid. *Christianity: The First Three Thousand Years*. New York: Viking, 2009.

McLynn, Frank. *Richard and John: Kings at War*. Cambridge, MA: DaCapo, 2007.

Mitchel, Kathleen. "Clovis I." https://www.britannica.com/biography/Clovis-I.

Neveux, Francois. *A Brief History of the Normans: The Conquests That Changed the Face of Europe*. Translated by Howard Curtis. London: Robinson, 2006.

Richardson, Don. *Lords of the Earth*. Ventura, CA: Regal, 1977.

_____. *Peace Child*. Glendale, CA: Regal, 1974.

Walker, Williston. *A History of the Christian Church*. New York: Charles Scribner's Sons, 1959.

Wasson, Donald L. "Clovis I." https://www.ancient.eu/Clovis_I/.

Watkins, Oscar Daniel. *A History of Penance, Being a Study of Authorities (a) For the Whole Church to A.D. 450, (b) For the Western Church from A.D. 450 to A.D. 1215*. 2 vols. London: Longmans, Green, and Co., 1920.

Biblical Studies

Botterweck, G. Johannes et. al., eds. *Theological Dictionary of the Old Testament*. Translated by John T. Willis. Grand Rapids: Eerdmans, 1975.

Bush, Frederic. *Word Biblical Commentary: Ruth/Esther*. Dallas: Word, 1996.

Dodd, C.H. *The Apostolic Preaching and Its Developments*. Grand Rapids: Baker, 1980.

_____. *The Epistle of Paul to the Romans*. New York: Harper and Row.

Dunn, James D.G. *Word Biblical Commentary: Romans 1–8*. Dallas: Word, 1988.

Durham, John I. *Word Biblical Commentary: Exodus*. Dallas: Word, 1987.

Grosheide, F.W. *The New International Commentary on the New Testament. Commentary on the First Epistle to the Corinthians*. Grand Rapids: Eerdmans, 1953.

Hagner, Donald A. *Word Biblical Commentary: Matthew 1–13* and *Matthew 14–28*. Dallas: Word, 1993, 1995.

Handford, S.A. *Langenscheidt's Pocket Latin Dictionary: Latin-English*. New York: Barnes and Noble, 1961.

Harris. R. Laird et al., eds. *Theological Wordbook of the Old Testament*. Chicago: Moody, 1980.

Abba, *Father*

Hill, David. *Greek Words and Hebrew Meanings: Studies in the Semantics of Theological Terms.* Eugene, OR: Wipf and Stock, 1967.
Lane, William L. *The New International Commentary on the New Testament: The Gospel According to Mark.* Edited by F.F. Bruce. Grand Rapids: Eerdmans, 1974.
Longenecker, Richard N. *Word Biblical Commentary: Galatians.* Dallas: Word, 1990.
Kittel, Gerhard, ed. *Theological Dictionary of the New Testament.* Translated and edited by Geoffrey W. Bromiley. Grand Rapids: Eerdmans, 1967.
Lincoln, Andrew. *Word Biblical Commentary: Ephesians.* Dallas: Word, 1990.
Luther, Martin. *Commentary on Romans.* Translated by J. Theodore Mueller. Grand Rapids: Kregel, 1954.
Melick, Richard E. *The New American Commentary.* Vol. 32, *Philippians, Colossians, Philemon.* Nashville: Broadman, 1991.
Michael, J. Ramsey. *Word Biblical Commentary.* Vol. 49, *1 Peter.* Waco: Word, 1988.
Morris, Leon. *The Apostolic Preaching of the Cross.* Grand Rapids: Eerdmans, 1956.
Murray, John. *The New International Commentary on the New Testament. The Epistle to the Romans.* Grand Rapids: Eerdmans, 1959, 1965.
Nygren, Anders. *Commentary on Romans.* Translated by Carl C. Rasmussen. Philadelphia: Fortress, 1949.
Oden, Thomas C., gen. ed. *Ancient Christian Commentary on Scripture: New Testament.* 12 vols. Downers Grove, IL: IVP, 1998–2005.
Sanday, William and Arthur C. Headlam. *The International Critical Commentary. A Critical and Exegetical Commentary on the Epistle to the Romans.* 5th ed. Edinburgh: T.&T. Clark, 1907.
Shanks, Hershel, ed. *Christianity and Rabbinic Judaism.* Biblical Archaeology Society, 1992.
_____. *Partings: How Judaism and Christianity Became Two.* Washington, DC: Biblical Archaeology Society, 2013.
Tonstad, Sigve. *The Revisionary Potential of "Abba! Father!" in the Letters of Paul.* Andrews University Seminary Studies, vol. 45, no. 1, 5-18. Berrien Springs, MI: Andrews University Press, 2007.
Wright, N.T. *New Interpreter's Bible.* Vol. 10, "Romans." Nashville: Abingdon, 2002.

Theology

Anselm, *Cur Deus Homo.* Written in 1097. Translated by Sidney Norton Deane, 1903. Columbia, SC: Pantianos, 2016.
Athanasius. *On the Incarnation.* Translated and edited by A Religious of C.S.M.V. S.Th. Louisville, KY: GLH Publishing, 2018.
Aulen, Gustaf. *Christus Victor.* Translated by A.G. Hebert. New York: MacMillan, 1969.
_____. *The Faith of the Christian Church.* Translated by Eric H. Wahlstrom. London: SCM Press, 1960.
Browning, Don S. *Atonement and Psychotherapy.* Philadelphia: Westminster, 1966.
Calvin, John. *Calvin: Commentaries.* Edited by Joseph Haroutunian. The Library of Christian Classics. Philadelphia: Westminster, 1958.
_____. *Institutes of the Christian Religion.* 5 editions, 1536–1559. Translated by Henry Beveridge. Peabody, MA: Hendrikson, 2008. [Book 2, chs. 12–16]
Campbell, John McLeod. *The Nature of the Atonement and Its Relation to Remission of Sins and Eternal Life.* Cambridge: MacMillan, 1856.

Finlan, Stephen. *Problems with Atonement: The Origins of, and Controversy about, the Atonement Doctrine.* Collegeville, MN: Liturgical Press, 2005.

_____. *Salvation Not Purchased: Overcoming the Ransom Idea to Rediscover the Original Gospel Teaching.* Eugene, OR: Cascade, 2020.

_____. *The Family Metaphor in Jesus Teaching: Gospel Imagery and Application.* 2nd ed. Eugene, OR: Cascade, 2013.

Forsyth, P.T. *The Work of Christ.* London: Independent Press, 1910.

Hall, Thor. *Makers of the Modern Theological Mind: Anders Nygren.* Waco: Word, 1978.

Hefling, Charles. "Why the Cross? God's At-One-Ment with Humanity." *The Christian Century,* (March 11, 2013). https://www.christiancentury.org/article/2013-02/why-cross.

Humphreys, Fisher. *The Death of Christ.* Nashville: Broadman, 1978.

Humphreys, Fisher and Paul E. Robertson. *God So Loved the World: Traditional Baptists and Calvinism.* New Orleans: Insight, 2000.

Kelly, J.N.D. *Early Christian Doctrines.* New York: Harper and Row, 1958, 1960.

Lucado, Max. *No Wonder They Call Him the Savior.* Nashville: Thomas Nelson, 1986, 2004.

Nygren, Anders. "The Atonement as a Work of God." In *Essence of Christianity, Two Essays.* 81-128. Grand Rapids: Eerdmans, 1960.

Packer, J.I. "What Did the Cross Achieve? The Logic of Penal Substitution." *Tyndale Bulletin* 25 (1974): 3-45. https://legacy.tyndalehouse.com/tynbul/Library/TynBull_1974_25_01_Pakcer_CrossAchieve.pdf.

Rashdall, Hastings. *The Idea of the Atonement in Christian Theology: Being the Bampton Lectures for 1915.* London: Macmillan, 1920. Reprint Miami: HardPress.

Roberts, Alexander and James Donaldson, eds. *The Ante-Nicene Fathers.* Vols. 1–4. American Reprint of the Edinburgh Edition. Grand Rapids: Eerdmans, 1967–1969.

Stott, John R.W. *The Cross of Christ.* Downers Grove, IL: IVP, 2006.

Stump, Eleonore. *Atonement.* Oxford: University Press, 2018.

Tertullian. *On the Flesh of Christ,* in *The Ante-Nicene Fathers.* III. *Latin Christianity: Its Founder, Tertullian.* Edited by Alexander Roberts and James Donaldson. Grand Rapids: Eerdmans, 1968.

_____. *De Fuga in Persecutione,* in *The Ante-Nicene Fathers.* IV. *Fathers of the Third Century.* Edited by Alexander Roberts and James Donaldson. Grand Rapids: Eerdmans, 1968.

Tillich, Paul. *Systematic Theology.* 3 vols in 1. Chicago: University of Chicago, 1951, 1957, 1963.

Torrey, R.A., et. al eds. *The Fundamentals.* 4 vols. Originally published by The Bible Institute of Los Angeles, 1917. Reprinted Grand Rapids: Baker, 2000.
- Chap. 5. "The Atonement," Franklin Johnson, 64–77.
- Chap. 6. "At-One-Ment, By Propitiation," Dyson Hague, 78–97.
- Chap. 7. "The Grace of God," C.I. Scofield, 98–109.
- Chap. 8. "Salvation by Grace," Thomas Spurgeon, 110–127.

Turner, H.E.W. *The Patristic Doctrine of Redemption: A Study of the Development of Doctrine During the First Five Centuries.* London: A.R. Mowbray, 1952.

www.ingramcontent.com/pod-product-compliance
Lightning Source LLC
Chambersburg PA
CBHW071006160426
43193CB00012B/1936